PROBING THE SPIRIT

A Theological Evaluation of Communal Discernment

LADISLAS ORSY, S.J.

Dimension Books, Inc.
Denville, New Jersey

Second and Revised Edition
Published by Dimension Books, Inc.
Denville, New Jersey 07834

ACKNOWLEDGEMENTS

Probing the Spirit is the revised and enlarged edition of an essay first published under the title, "Toward a Theological Evaluation of Communal Discernment" in *Studies in the Spirituality of Jesuits.* The present edition also contains a new section on the relationship between authority and discernment.

We thank the members of the Seminar for advising us in the preparation of the first edition and in particular Father George E. Ganss, S.J., director of the Seminar, for permitting the use of this material for our second edition of this work.

TABLE OF CONTENTS

FOREWORD

To probe the ways of the spirit is an adventure out of the ordinary, an enterprise that is fascinating and humiliating, all at once.

It is an adventure out of the ordinary because it is far easier to look outward than to look inward. The universe that surrounds us holds our attention with its display of movements, sounds and colors. To find the ways of the spirit we must turn in the opposite direction, we must enter a world of silence and mystery. Once there, we become aware of new signs of life that speak about the source of all life.

To experience inwardly even fragmentary manifestations of God's power and glory is a fascinating event for any human being; it lifts him up beyond his expectation, and it humiliates him against his desire. It reveals God's greatness and goodness; it bares his poverty and weakness.

In our title the term 'spirit' is used ambivalently. It may mean the Spirit of God; it may mean the spirit of man. We apologize for such confusion but there is a good precedent for it. Saint Paul in his Epistles more than once refers to the 'spirit,' leaving it to the reader to find out if he speaks of the Spirit of God, or the spirit of man, or both.

After all, even if the two are distinct, they cannot be separated without doing violence to both. Through gentle grace, our human spirit became the dwelling place of the Spirit of God.

Epiphany, 1976.

INTRODUCTION

A MULTITUDE OF THEORETICAL PROBLEMS

The attempt to evaluate community discernment is a search for the correct theological description or definition of it. Once we know its nature with some precision, we shall be in a good position to determine what we can or cannot expect from it, and also what our practical attitudes should be toward it.

But in the field of theological reflection no question stands alone; each is linked to many others as closely as the arches of a Gothic cathedral are bound together. No one of them can be pulled out and examined separately. It would have no meaning outside of its place; besides, its removal would endanger the whole building.

The innocent question "What is community discernment?," is linked up with momentous theological problems over which theologians have battled for centuries, often with no better result than an admission that they were in the presence of a mystery that their minds could not penetrate.

Indeed, the search for the understanding of community discernment is a search into mysteries. Some examples easily demonstrate the truth of this statement.

1. Community discernment is usually described as a method of finding God's will through the move-

ments of grace in the inner being of the participants. But such a search cannot be explained in theological terms unless the much broader question of the relationship between divine gifts and human capacities is faced. On the one hand, we Christians are children of light with an ability to perceive the presence of divine mysteries and to receive divine life itself. On the other hand, we are earthly creatures with a mortal body and limited intelligence.

Can we identify God's gifts with precision? Are we able to say what comes from our resources? If we cannot answer these questions with quiet certainty, how can we speak about discovering God's mind and will? Indeed, to know how much the community can accomplish in the process of discernment, we should have a good knowledge about the relationship between God's gifts and man's capacity to receive them.

2. This leads us to the kindred question of the relationship between God's grace and man's freedom. After the Dominicans and Jesuits had been entrapped in a futile battle for centuries by wrongly formulated questions, they finally came to the realization that the issue is more mysterious than it appeared to either of the two sides. After all, who can tell exactly how far the good deeds of a Christian proceed from divine initiative or how far they have their source in human freedom? To understand the discernment process, we should know more about the respective roles of grace and freedom in making a decision.

3. If we knew God's providence in all its intricacies, it would be much easier for us to handle the meaning of community discernment. But we have no such knowledge. All that we can do is to sound some warnings. The "will of God" is one of the most

complex terms in systematic theology. It can mean God's positive and efficacious will: he does what he wants. "For who can resist his will?" (Rm 9:19). It can mean his permissive will, which allows evil to operate in this universe: he does not want any evil, yet he allows his creatures to revolt against his design. "For God has consigned all men to disobedience, that he may have mercy upon all" (Rm 11:32). Between these two meanings of the term "God's will," there are many others. In any particular situation positive and permissive wills may be present in different combinations. How can a community sort them all out?

4. There is the problem of interpreting the present will of God in relation to his future design. On the one side, there is the naive conception that God has a special blueprint for our lives in all details, and that we have the duty to discover it and make it into the norm of our actions. On the other side, there is the simplistic belief that God leaves us fully autonomous, and that we decide the course of our life as we wish it. In truth, our God is neither the meticulous and oppressive planner, nor the distant and cool observer. He is a friend with great love who respects our freedom but has also his dreams about our future. How to bring these two aspects together in harmonious concepts? Fortunately, good Christians who know no theoretical solution to this problem have the faith to reach out for the guiding hand of a friend, and have the courage to accept responsibility for their own actions. They do not fail in their expectations.

5. At a somewhat different level, there is the question of how infused contemplation works in man's heart. The best spiritual writers are in agreement in saying that the gift of wisdom—and discern-

ment is a species of wisdom—is a gift akin to that of infused contemplation. Even if such gifts are given radically with the baptismal grace, they are not very often found in their fullness in adult Christians. How far, then, can the contemplative gift of discernment be presumed to exist in the members of an ordinary community? The right understanding of community discernment may well depend on the answer to such questions.

6. In the Church of Corinth, however, Paul found gifts and charisms among ordinary folk who were not very different from what Christians are today; therefore, a good Christian community must have the necessary wisdom for discernment! Especially if we judge those Corinthians by their faults as well as their graces, both of which were amply described by the apostle. Precious gifts existed in that community side by side with serious deficiencies. How do we explain such contrasts? Was the community composed of persons of very different calibre, one saint, the other sinner? Or did divine gifts exist side by side with human failures in the same persons? What conclusions can we draw for ourselves? We are not in a position to give a well-reasoned answer.

Problems in the field of theory, indeed abound. Solutions are hard to come by. But every right question is a real step toward progress, even if the answer is not evident or complete.

Fortunately the gifts of the Spirit do not depend on our reflections. They are given before we can analyze them; gifts precede reflections. Neither should prayerful deliberations depend on abstract explanations. While theologians are working their way toward a conceptual understanding, communities that are one in mind and heart should go on praying to find out how they should take the next step in the service of the Lord. The praise of God and the work for his Kingdom should never be delayed because we are not ready with our scholarly articulations.

The Lord said: "For everyone who asks receives, and he who seeks finds, and to him who knocks it will be opened" (Mt 7:8). Community discernment is a way of asking, seeking and knocking. Its method may be different from community to community; the Lord leaves all free to follow what is the best for them. The overriding truth is that when the community gathers in prayer, the Risen Lord is with his disciples again. The best fruit of any discernment will be always the recognition of his presence, as it was given to the disciples at Emmaus: "They said to each other, 'Did not our hearts burn within us while he talked to us on the road, while he opened to us the scriptures?' " (Lk 24:32).

FIVE QUESTIONS

We religious have made much progress in recent years in understanding the nature and working of our communities. Each community is an organic body; it is alive when there is a dynamic interplay among the members. It must have a center where one (or several) persons clothed with authority stand, and to whom informational data flow steadily from all directions. The task of the center is to create one mind and one heart in the community, out of the multiplicity of ideas and desires, in harmony with the aspirations of

[11]

the universal Church. Such organic unity among intelligent persons cannot arise if those in authority alone decide all issues and call for unconditional and blind surrender in others. The ones who preside must respond in a spirit of service to the right and just desires of all.

From such an understanding of religious community, new decision-making processes have sprung up. Communal discernment is the most important among them. Some communities are practicing it; some are puzzled by it; all want to know more about it. To satisfy the need several studies have been published on the topic, a few of them are listed in the bibliography at the end of this volume. They helped and continue to help many. Indeed, groups once locked into insoluble conflicts are now praying and searching together to find the will of God; groups once gripped by despair are freed by newly-found hope. The fruit produced tells the quality of the seed.

Since the studies, especially those published in English, were responding to an urgent need, their orientation was mainly practical. They raised the question: How can a community seek and find the will of God? They proposed a rather well-defined pattern of method to find the answer.

The time has now come to raise the question more explicitly, especially from the viewpoint of theological investigation: What is communal discernment? This is the purpose of this study. For the sake of clarity and orderliness, it will unfold around five specific queries.

First, what are the theological foundations of communal discernment?

Second, what are the legitimate expectations that the discernment process can fulfill?

Third, what expectations are not legitimate; in

other terms, what is it that the community cannot obtain through discernment?

Fourth, what is the relationship between authority and community discernment?

Fifth, what practical guidelines follow from our theological considerations?

In exploring these questions, we gather our reflections around thirty-five theses or propositions.

FIRST QUESTION: WHAT ARE THE THEOLOGICAL FOUNDATIONS OF COMMUNAL DISCERNMENT?

DISCERNMENT REQUIRES CONTEMPLATIVE INSIGHT

1. Communal discernment in its best and purest form is the articulation of a contemplative insight into the working of God's grace in a community.

We say in its best and purest form because we have to begin there. Wholeness is the clue to the understanding of the fragments. Contemplative insight means knowledge obtained not so much by human effort and creativity as through God's gracious gift; a knowledge akin to the "intimate understanding and relish of the truth" (*el sentir y gustar de las cosas internamente*) of which St. Ignatius speaks in his *Exercises* [2] and which plays such an important role in them. Such knowledge is discovered, appropriated and authenticated through consolations from God, such as are peace, joy and encouragement; it is certainly not the logical outcome of a reasoning

[13]

process. We may even say that community discernment is the discovery of a gift by another gift; the discovery of God's plan for the community through the light of faith infused into the minds of the members. In other and more biblical terms: it is the recognition of God's sometimes scandalous or foolish ways, "a stumbling block to Jews and folly to Gentiles" (1 Co 1:23), through the presence of the fruits of the Spirit: "love, joy, peace, patience, kindness, goodness, faithfulness, gentleness, self-control" (Ga 5:22-23).

In this process there is an interplay between two poles. One is the plan of God to be known, the other is the human spirit that reaches out for it and intends to articulate it in some conceptual form. To become aware of this interplay between two poles is a fundamental requirement for the understanding and consequently for the right use of the process. There is God's hidden mystery on the one side, there is man who perceives it on the other side.

No wonder that such discernment requires contemplative persons, well-versed in finding God's presence by instinct. A sensitivity to the gentle movements of grace is necessary to the point of being an indispensable condition. Without it there is no wholeness in discernment.

INSIGHT INTO GOD'S WAYS

> **2. Discernment in its fullest religious sense is about truly great spiritual issues, where neither the simplicity of the dove nor the cleverness of the serpent is enough.**

[14]

Obviously enough, if discernment is a contemplative insight into God's own ways, it should be used mainly for those issues that cannot be solved in any other way, that is by ordinary prayerful investigation and reasoning. Then, discernment is indeed necessary: "For my thoughts are not your thoughts, neither are your ways my ways, says the Lord. For as the heavens are higher than the earth, so are my ways higher than your ways and my thoughts than your thoughts" (Is 55:8-9). Only God can give an insight into his own plan, only he can confirm a decision that is the fruit of an attraction by the Father: "No one can come to me unless the Father who sent me draws him" (Jn 6:44).

AN EARLY EXAMPLE: THE APOSTOLIC COUNCIL OF JERUSALEM

3. Communal discernment itself (as distinguished from the terminology) is not new in the Church; a careful reading of the acts of the Apostolic Council of Jerusalem reveals all of its essential elements (Ac 15:1-35).

The Apostolic Council of Jerusalem was concerned with great religious issue involving the future of the whole Church: were the Gentiles asking for baptism obliged to take circumcision as well? In other words, does salvation come through the Law and its practices, as the party of the Pharisees contended, or does it come through the grace of the Lord Jesus alone as Paul claimed it?

If we consider the strength of the Jewish tradition and how the Church of Jesus grew out of that

[15]

tradition, we can understand that the issue was not a small one. Mere reasoning and logic could not solve it. After all, did not the Master come to uphold and perfect the Law? (Mt 5:17). Admittedly, he insisted also that the sabbath was for man and that all nations are invited into the Kingdom. But among those apparently conflicting testimonies, how could the apostles decide without the light of the Spirit? There had to be discernment in the full sense.

The apostles gathered together with the elders and disciples. The core of the assembly was the small group which prayed together in that upper room when the Spirit of the Lord was poured out on them. No doubt as they met to deliberate, they were united in prayer again as only they could be. Today in more prosaic language we would say that they put themselves into the right disposition before God, or they made themselves "indifferent" or impartial. More correctly we should say that they allowed God to dispose their hearts for the truth.

Luke describes how arguments were brought up from both sides. But interestingly enough, the disciples did not much debate the merits of the question. They spoke about the witness of the Holy Spirit who cleansed the hearts of many and worked signs and wonders among them. The party of the Pharisees, then Peter, then Barnabas and Paul, all said their piece.

There was silence in the assembly during the speeches. "And all the assembly kept silence; and they listened to Barnabas and Paul as they related what signs and wonders God had done through them among the Gentiles" (Ac 15:12). They listened. Is this not what we call openness to all sides and willingness to opt for wisdom instead of narrow prejudice?

[16]

Finally James gave a summing up and proposed a solution that was based on the words of the prophets, on the signs of the times, and on some shrewd wisdom that made him opt for new ways, yet not without granting some concessions to the older ones. "Therefore my judgment is that we should not trouble those of the Gentiles who turn to God, but should write to them to abstain from the pollutions of idols and from unchastity and from what is strangled and from blood" (Ac 15:19-20).

James' wisdom paved the way for a consensus. The participants were able to formulate a message approved by them all. It included the words that later became familiar to readers of the documents of ecumenical councils. "For it has seemed good to the Holy Spirit and to us" (Ac 15:28), *placuit Spiritui sancto et nobis*: a proclamation that the decision is not so much the logical conclusion of a debate carefully conducted as the discovery of a new light given by the Spirit.

The Acts report that when the letter was communicated to the Church of Antioch, "they rejoiced at the exhortation" (15:31). There was peace in the congregation. The fruits of the Spirit sealed the decision.

Admittedly we do not claim that the acts of the Apostolic Council of Jerusalem displayed the same neat and organized procedure that is found in the communal discernment process as it is practiced in many places today. But the gist of it all is there.

The biblical precedent gives us a broader horizon. We know that we are not joining a movement of dubious origins. We follow a route traced by the apostles. Such historical awareness helps us to realize that ever since the Council of Jerusalem, communal discernment has been practiced in the Church whenever men and women graced by God came together and set out to search for those high thoughts and ways of the Lord that no man can know through his own efforts alone.

LATER DEVELOPMENTS: COUNCILS AND RELIGIOUS GROUPS

4. Throughout the long history of the Church, there were outstanding examples of community discernment; the most important ones occurred in ecumenical councils and in religious communities, especially at the time of their foundation.

The community of bishops, assembled in councils, universal or particular, had to discern the meaning of God's word. They were aware that their canons, decrees and "determinations" were more than the fruit of human calculations and conjectures: they were insights into a mystery. Because of this belief, the bishops could say with authenticity: "it seemed good to the Holy Spirit and to us": *placuit Spiritui sancto et nobis.*

Moreover, it is legitimate to assume that discernment was a way of life for early monastic communities, be it in the East or in the West. Originally the monastery harbored a small fervent group seeking to find the will of God through prayer and penance under the leadership of the abbot. There can be little doubt that the monastic chapter with its prayerful atmosphere and subdued discussion grew out of a common effort to seek and find the will of God in all things; that is, of a regular exercise of communal discernment.

[18]

The early history of the great mendicant orders, Franciscans and Dominicans, would offer several examples of community discernment especially while the community was in the process of formation, or was working on the formulation of rules and constitutions.

Into this enduring tradition must be inserted the practice of communal discernment used by St. Ignatius and his first companions. As Ignatius did not invent the discernment of spirits but set some good practical rules for doing it, the first Jesuits did not invent communal discernment but left the records of an orderly way of doing it.

THE FIRST FATHERS OF THE SOCIETY OF JESUS

> **5. The process through which Saint Ignatius and his first companions arrived at the decision to form a religious community is a good model of communal discernment.**

The early history of the Jesuits provides an outstanding example of communal discernment. The process has been carefully recorded by one of the group, in the document known as the *Deliberatio primorum Patrum*, somewhat freely translated by "Deliberation of the Founding Fathers."

The conditions required for genuine discernment were verified in this group of ten. There was a Spirit-filled community. For years the members of the group had lived the *Exercises* with all its divine consolations and human harshness. They were guided by Ignatius who was blessed with extraordinary

[19]

mystical graces well beyond our comprehension.

They faced a great spiritual issue, important not only for them but for the universal Church: should they form a permanent organic body, a religious order in fact, where the bond of unity would be obedience; or, should they remain as they were, dear friends in the Lord, but with no permanent bond among them? If ever an issue had to be discerned by the criteria of the *Exercises*, through consolations and desolations, this was the one. Fortunately, the persons were equal to the task.

After months of prayer and discussion, these "pilgrim priests" decided to form a permanent union, and the Society of Jesus was born. History has proved their spiritual insight. They discovered the intrinsic trust of grace in their midst.

SOME HISTORICAL QUESTIONS ABOUT THE FIRST TEN JESUITS

6. The message for our time coming from the early historical records of the Society of Jesus on discernment cannot be grasped accurately until the usual hermeneutical process of interpretation is completed and the past events are understood within their historical context.

To understand what happened, we must search for the sixteenth century meaning of the records; we should not project our own modern ideas into them. To draw practical conclusions for our times, we must go through a rigorous process of historical criticism. Any deviation from this basic rule leads to distortion of both our knowledge of past history and the soundness of present practice.

Obviously this historical reconstruction cannot take place here. It would require a full-fledged study. Yet some pertinent questions can be and must be raised here to make us aware of the historical dimensions of the problems, and in particular of the need for a well-grounded hermeneutical process that enables us to transpose, from old times into new ones, the values contained in the records.

How Far Did Ignatius Inspire the Group?

To understand the nature of this deliberation of the ten companions, we must ask to what extent the decision of the small group to accept mission from one of them—that is, to form a religious order in the classical sense—emerged from the group, and to what extent it came from Ignatius. Did they all, Ignatius included, begin their deliberation from the same state of ignorance, doubt and detachment, or was one of them, Ignatius, in possession of an extraordinary vision that helped him to enlighten his companions throughout the deliberation and to raise their minds and hearts to the internal knowledge and aspiration that he possessed? This is a fundamental question. If the final decision emerged fully from the group, their deliberation must be described as a truly creative process in which each played a role and played it equally, even if each made a different contribution. If, however, Ignatius entered the process with a vision and with a gentle and quiet assurance that God wanted him to be an instrument to enlighten his companions, then the decision originated more in one person than in many. In the first hypothesis, all

[21]

would have contributed equally throughout the process. In the second, the group would have gradually appropriated the vision of its leader.

We do not propose here any definite answer, but we assert that there are good reasons to investigate the matter. A whole series of events in the life of Ignatius indicate an increasing desire to gather companions around himself and to form a group permanently united in the service of the Church. His painful search to find companions, marked by failures first and eminent successes later, had all the dynamics toward organizing a group that would stay together. To assume that Ignatius entered this process of deliberation without a vision of permanent unity in the group, in a state of blank indifference about its outcome, is to ignore the history and the dynamics of his life after his conversion in 1521. To assume that he had a vision which he wanted to communicate to his companions who had received the same graces in the same abundance makes good historical sense. It is in harmony with the trend of Ignatius' life from his conversion to the deliberation of 1539.

Our aim here is not to decide this issue. We submit simply that the nature of this first discernment cannot be stated correctly as long as this historical question is not answered. To answer it, detailed research is necessary in all the documents in order to reconstruct, as far as possible, the mind of Ignatius in the beginning of this deliberation. In one way or another, the answer will shed light on what the deliberations were: either a groping from darkness to light in all the companions, or the communication to all, by means of prayerful considerations, of the light which had been previously given to one.

Obviously, we are aware that the word "indif-

ference" has various meanings. One of them, uncon-
cern about either alternative, is not applicable here.
In the context of the *Deliberatio,* another sense
would be an indifference which does not as yet
include any vision of, or attraction to a determined
goal, but is ready to accept whatever is revealed
throughout the process as God's will. Still another
sense would be an indifference which means that a
person does have such a vision or attraction, but is
ready to sacrifice it if God should indicate that to be
his will. Our question is: Precisely in what sense was
Ignatius indifferent to the outcome of the deliberation?

Why Did Ignatius Later Prescribe Other Methods?

Furthermore, before a model is widely copied, it is
necessary to assess what in the model is the expression of unique and particular circumstances, and what
is destined to be the standard pattern for general use.
Ignatius himself displayed discretion in drawing up
plans for any future discernment process. In the
Constitutions [694-718], he gives fairly detailed rules
for the election of the General and for transacting
business at General Congregations. In neither case is
the pattern of the "Deliberation of the Founding
Fathers" reproduced. Sudden inspirations from the
Holy Spirit are certainly allowed, for elections and
decisions can be made by acclamation, that is, by one
common acceptance of a powerful movement of the
Spirit. But ordinarily elections and decisions are made
through the humble means of votes given and
counted; and the history of the Society of Jesus does
not report the use of any other method than this

[23]

ordinary one. Never in their history, have Jesuits elected a Superior General by unanimous acclamation. Why did Ignatius, one of the greatest masters of discernment in the history of the Christian Church, prescribe such ordinary means? Did he look at the method of communal discernment used by the First Fathers as somewhat unique, to be used for exceptional issues, by persons equal in grace and wisdom to that small group? Or, and this is another possibility, did Ignatius perceive the core of discernment in the discovery of a grace that can be reached in many ways and by many means, including that of counting the votes? In other terms, did he distinguish between the theological event of recognizing a grace and a certain external process that prepares for it? The recognition would be necessary in all historical situations, but the practical method of achieving it could be changed as occasion demands.

How Should the Rules for Discernment of Spirits
   Be Applied to Communities?

The transfer of the "Rules for the Discernment of Spirits" (*Exercises,* [313-336]), conceived for individual spiritual direction, into community situations is a complex process. Each person remains unique even when he is a member of a community; yet the community is one through a bond that transcends all individual differences. Each person must be given the respect that is due to an intelligent and free child of God, yet the common mind and the common will of the group must be taken into account. Delicate balances are necessary to satisfy the demands of both sides, and to bring about the desired harmony between the two. Those balances cannot be fixed by permanent and static measures; they must shift and change, bringing into the fore the uniqueness of the person at one time, the common mind and common heart at another time.

How should this adaptation be accomplished? The answer may be easier in practice than in theory. But unless we are able to formulate guidelines based on sound theology, sooner or later some communities will be misled by a combination of good will and theological ignorance. If the right balance is not achieved, either the person will suffer, or the common spirit will be destroyed.

All these issues demand critical inquiry in depth. But it does not follow that while the work of historical and theological investigation goes on, communal discernment should stop. Enough valid insights have already emerged to guide wise men and women in search of progress in God's service, provided they are conscious that there is still much to be learned.

DISCERNMENT IN OUR DAYS

> 7. Communal discernment is a good instrument of progress for lesser giants than Ignatius and his companions, and for lesser issues than the founding of a new religious community, provided that from beginning to end the members of the discerning group are aware of their limitations.

Two principles are implied in this statement, both fairly obvious. One says that the more remote a person is from contemplative insight, the less he should presume that he is able to discover infallibly

[25]

the movement of grace in a community. The other tells us that no extraordinary illumination should be expected from the Spirit when the ordinary use of human intelligence assisted by grace is enough to decide an issue. That is, communal discernment will be an instrument of progress for humble folk who know their own limits. For others, it will become rapid transport into a dreamworld filled with illusions. Let us see more closely, therefore, what discernment is in an ordinary community.

Community discernment for most of us means to form a common judgment or to make a common decision reached through a pattern of prayerful reflections to which all contribute. The process can be complex. Its result is more than the˙sum of individual judgments or decisions; the fruit is produced by all. The method requires the sharing of all available data, the articulation of insights into the known facts, the formulation of definite judgments, and the making of decisions. It includes even more an alertness to the movements of grace in each person throughout the whole process. There is an interplay among the members; the community thinks, speaks, acts as an organic body where each is unique and yet united to the others.

The right understanding of this "communion in action" lies between two extreme conceptions. One exalts the unity of the community to the point that respect due to persons is destroyed; the other stresses the individual differences so far that the community vanishes in the process. Both are wrong; the truth is in the middle: all human beings are persons who find their fulfillment in a community. To be a person is to have the highest dignity in this creation. A person has intelligence and freedom. Also, he has a right to develop according to his own pace, to his own internal light, even in community. Ultimately all data, all information are received by the individual mind; all insights that bring meaning into them are generated by the individual intelligence; all judgments that confess the truth must be made personally; and all decisions for good or evil must spring from personal responsibility. Each person remains autonomous throughout the process of communal discernment.

Yet no person exists alone; he must be integrated into a community. Integration is more than a loose association among many. It is a new, mysterious unity in which the personhood of each remains but it is enriched by all the others. The information gathered by each becomes the property of all; insights into facts are shared, judgments are construed through mutual help, and finally, options are chosen as inspired by a common ideal.

We do not claim to understand fully the situation of an intelligent and free person in community. But we know that the primacy of the person must be affirmed even in a community. Otherwise, the highest dignity in creation would be diminished and its gifts diffused in some kind of collectivity. There is no situation in which a person should renounce the use of his intelligence and freedom. Yet those who form a community can do much to enhance mutually the operation of their intelligence and freedom even to the point that they all come to a similar judgment and take the same decision; that is, they become of one mind and of one heart. Such unity is all the more possible when they take their inspiration from the same sources: from the Gospels and the teaching of the Christian Church; and when they are assisted by the same mysterious strength that comes from the Spirit of God.

[27]

Communal discernment can be fruitful only if the integrity of the Christian person who is existing and operating in a community is respected. The community can never take away the intelligence and the freedom of the individual; but it can do much to guide him within the limits of prudence to avoid false judgments originating in a biased mind and to avoid wrong decisions stemming from misguided attachments. The community can create a climate of prayer to assure that grace and wisdom prevail over the pull of prejudices and of selfish interests. Besides, there is the mysterious action of the Spirit who can give the same vision to many and can strengthen the group for the same action.

Individuals who are unable to make autonomous judgments and independent decisions, those who are thrown about by every wind that blows in the community, are not fit to make a contribution toward a common judgment and decision since they have nothing to contribute.

It follows that communal discernment is for strong persons. Each must go through a thorough preparation, reflection and prayerful consideration, as if he had to decide the issue for himself. If the majority is weak or not well-prepared, one or two may carry the others with them. Then, there is no communal discernment, but discernment by some, after whom the others drift.

NO MEAN TASK

8. Communal discernment should be a process through which the community attempts to appropriate the best insight existing somewhere in the

members, and make it into the community's own
judgment. This is a correct description of what
ought to happen; although it may not happen
many times!

The community in the process of discernment
must be aware of the hard truth that no insight is
deeper, no judgment is better, just because many
have it or many make it. The number of contributors
in itself is no guarantee for quality. Yet many pairs of
eyes can see more than one. Those who participate in
the search can pool their information and help each
other in the movement that leads to new insights and
produces well-grounded judgments and decisions.

Indeed nothing less than the best judgment should
do. Communal discernment would defeat its own
purpose if sharp insights and well-founded judgments
are impeded or watered down to a common denomi-
nator acceptable to all. It follows that the internal
dynamics of deliberations ought to move toward the
highest vision and the most creative decisions that can
emerge from the group. No mean task!

This thesis should be especially stressed with
groups of religious men and women. The history of
religious communities shows how much the vision
and determination of one person inspired a new
movement and led many others to an intensely
dedicated life that otherwise they could not have
realized. It should be enough to mention such names
as Benedict, Francis, Dominic, Ignatius, Teresa of
Avila, John of the Cross, Vincent de Paul and so
many others. There is no historical evidence to show
that a large group of followers could have produced the same insight and could have shown the
same determinations as these men and women did.

[29]

There is a trend today spread over many fields, from politics to religion, that seems to believe that the correctness of a judgment or the rightness of a decision depends on the numbers that make it and not on the reasons that support it. Anyone familiar with any branch of human history knows that the best of insights never came too easily; that well-founded judgments were a rare commodity and total dedication to a good cause was a choice grace granted to a few.

GOD'S LIGHT AND MAN'S WEAKNESS

9. Ordinarily (not in its perfect form), communal discernment is a dynamic process in which the light and strength of God and the blurred vision of man all play their role. In it, a sinful community forms a judgment or makes a decision in God's luminous presence. The final result usually manifests something of all these ingredients.

In this mixture of contrasting elements is the clue to the understanding of the value of communal discernment. Through it the community meets with God, in a grace-filled atmosphere, and makes a step forward in the service of the Lord. The contrasts must' be there; they are the manifestation of our human condition. The members of the group are at various stages of their human and Christian development. Rightly so, since no one enters a religious order to put his holiness on display; rather, each comes to learn how to progress in accepting God's grace and in producing fruit in the exacting measure of the Gospels. Full wisdom and intelligence are not given overnight; differences in outlook, in understanding and in maturity remain.

[30]

Such differences play their role throughout the discernment process. While information regarding data can be publicized, not all participants can grasp it with the same breadth and depth. The communication of an insight is more difficult. Clues can be given, but the light that brings understanding must come from inside; it must be generated by the person concerned. No one can substitute for him. Also if someone is hampered by ' intellectual prejudices, ultimately he can be saved by himself only, no matter how much the community talks to him. Again, if one is the slave of a disordered attachment, he must liberate himself before he can make the right moral decision. He can receive powerful help but finally he is the moral agent who must act.

The techniques of discernment, such as, all participants focusing on one side of the issue first and on the other side second, are concerned with the right balance among various contributions in the process. Yet no technique can ever do justice to all the differences that follow from the distinction of persons. Happen what may, throughout the process, the individual must remain his whole self. To fall under the spell of some fascination, or to become the victim of some pressure in order to avoid a discordant note is to fall into a situation all the more dangerous because it has the appearance of harmony.

These statements should be understood and interpreted in the general context of the delicate relationship between person and community which we explained above. We do not imply even remotely that a person should not be integrated into a community, or that a whole community could not be under the powerful action of the Spirit which eventually brings fruit beyond the expectation and the capacity of each.

[31]

DISTINCTION BETWEEN SUBSTANCE AND PROCEDURE

10. The correct theological meaning of discernment is in the perception or discovery of a movement of grace, although the term is often used to include the procedural technique that best disposes a person for such discovery.

The use of the same term in these two different senses is justified, provided the respective meanings are clarified. Discernment in its proper sense means to perceive or to recognize an inspiration of grace. This correct, full meaning should be retained.

But no one is so pure that without any preparation he can focus on a divine gift. We come to God's presence from a long distance with a distracted mind, with a disturbed heart. Hence, we need to go through a process that cleanses our vision to judge what is true and makes us free to choose what is right. The scope of procedural techniques is to assure this much needed purification. Their role can be so important that without them genuine discernment cannot even take place. To be open to all arguments for a cause, and to be open to all reasons against it, is to possess a natural equilibrium and to have a capacity to give due attention to everything. To make ourselves indifferent (in the Ignatian sense of impartial) to advantages or disadvantages on the right and on the left is to make ourselves sensitive to a variety of inspirations.

There can be several good techniques, but the act of discovering grace is one and undivided. Discernment is there. The preparatory process can be changed according to the needs of a community. The act of discovery is beyond any method.

The procedure used by those priests who decided to become the small Society of Jesus was a good way of organizing their search and their prayer toward the discovery of grace. It was an existential "heuristic structure," good but by no means unique.

To sum it up: we must be aware that discernment has different meanings. It may refer to the theological act of accepting a call from God. It may refer to a procedure that disposes us for hearing the voice of God.

THE DISCOVERY OF A GIFT— THE CREATION OF A DECISION

11. In a more subtle way another distinction can be drawn between two possible objects of discernment. It is a troublesome distinction, deceptively clear in theory, but always difficult to apply in practice.

There is a difference between a knowledge which only God can give (since it transcends our capacity even in our graced condition), and a knowledge that we can reach (since it is within the capacity of our own intelligence healed and strengthened by God's grace). Some examples will make this distinction clear.

No amount of prayerful reflection on Jesus' general teaching could have revealed to Peter that he, Peter, was the rock on which the Church was to be built. He had to be told. So the Gospels report this act of special election and its revelation to Peter. But obviously enough, Peter was capable of reaching many decisions with the ordinary help of grace as to how to fulfill his ministry. The Gospels do not suggest anywhere that an uninterrupted revelation from heaven was to be necessary for him to carry out the mandate of Jesus. Even if once he had to be prompted by a special vision to accept Cornelius into the Church!

Admittedly, this is Peter's individual case. We chose it because it shows the sharp contrast between a new knowledge conveyed by God and a knowledge arising from the grace-filled potentials of a Christian.

If the evangelical counsels are a gift from God to the Church, no one but the Holy Spirit can call a man to that way of life, or can inspire a group of men to form a new religious order. The light that leads into such a new state of life must be discovered. The discernment process ought to be, in that case, a path to discovery.

But the members of a community already consti-tuted may well wonder if they should open a new school. There are many considerations: the good of the children, the good of the parents, the good of a particular parish. Yet all counted, the members of the community have the resources to bring together intelligence and grace and to make a decision for themselves. To expect the Spirit to intervene by a special act of revelation would be to neglect God's ordinary gifts. From their own resources of grace and wisdom, the community should bring forth a good decision.

Another image may help us to understand the distinction. When the object of discernment is a new light that man can only receive, he must prostrate himself before God in fasting and prayer, ready to learn from above what he cannot know by himself. But when the object of discernment is a new decision which is to be made about created things, man must pray and move, by means of human resources common to God's children, toward a sensible, grace-filled determination. In the former case the final outcome is given to man; in the latter it is created by man.

The two attitudes are as different as the humble acceptance of a gift is different from the daring conception of a new adventure.

The difference is in the knowledge that results from discernment. In one case it is discovery; in the other case it is a sort of creation.

In the process leading up to this knowledge there need not be much difference. All the techniques of purification of mind and heart employed for the one are perfectly suitable for the other. But in one case we are dealing with revelation; in the other case we are contemplating creative action in a grace-filled universe. In the practical order the distinction is hardly ever so clear. The same issue may include both aspects. In most cases, we are dealing with a union of the sacred and the secular, the divine and the human, grace and nature.

Yet, in the practical order it is difficult to distinguish a specific call that comes from God as an extraordinary gift, from a decision that comes from man out of his ordinary resources of nature and grace. This practical difficulty may lead someone to question the theoretical correctness of our fundamental distinction. Yet the line between an unexpected intervention of God in a human life and the ordinary creativity of a good person should not be blurred. It gives the clue to the understanding of the call of Abram, of Moses, and of so many other prophets in the Old Testament. It makes it possible to explain, without diluting them, the words of Jesus to the apostles, "You did not choose me, but I chose you" (Jn 15:16). Moreover, a strong conviction has always existed in the Church that persons such as Francis of Assisi, Dominic Guzman, Ignatius of Loyola and Teresa of Avila received from God a specific mission that no amount of meditation and reflection could have revealed to them. In some mysterious way—God's ways are many—a mandate was given to them. A similar grace can be given to a community. A group of persons can receive a mission for the good of the Church.

We must insist on the fundamental importance of this distinction because the nature of an issue to be decided must determine the attitude of discerners at a deeper level than any method can reach. In one case the accent must be on humble petition and waiting for God's own time to reveal his thoughts, as Ignatius so wisely directs in the matter of election in the *Exercises* ". . .while one is engaged in the Spiritual Exercises, it is more suitable and much better that the Creator and Lord in person communicate himself to the devout soul in quest of the divine will, that he inflame it with his love and praise, and dispose it for the way in which it could better serve God in the future" [*Exercises*, 15].

In another case we must create a decision with the ordinary gifts of nature and grace, knowing that whatever the decision is, God will not fail to stand by his children even to the point of bringing good out of their mistakes.

[36]

SECOND QUESTION: WHAT ARE THE LEGITIMATE EXPECTATIONS FROM COMMUNAL DISCERNMENT?

To find what are the reasonable and legitimate expectations from communal discernment, two further questions must be asked: (1) What can a community intent on discernment expect from the Lord? and (2) What can the community achieve in searching for his will?

These two questions should not be separated too sharply. The first simply points out that there are gifts that no man can conquer by force. They can come only through the gracious goodness of the Lord. The second question implies that there are decisions that man, enlightened by faith, strengthened by hope, and prompted by love, can make.

THE PRESENCE OF THE RISEN LORD

12. For a community intent on praying, the most legitimate expectation is the presence of the Risen Lord.

It is legitimate to expect the presence and the strength of the Lord among those who come together in his name. He himself promised it: "again, I say to you, if two of you agree on earth about anything they ask, it will be done for them by my Father in heaven. For where two or three are gathered in my

[37]

name, there am I in the midst of them" (Mt 18:19-20). The success of this prayer, of course, presupposes a community that lives by faith and love, and is not disturbed too much by earthly desires and dissensions.

When the community comes together, the Lord is with it. His presence is dynamic and purifying, eventually leading it in the right way; that is, to the expectation of the Kingdom and all that it implies.

The presence of the Lord is quiet and strong. It does not work wonders and miracles overnight, but it gives wisdom and strength to the members.

In fact, to come together for community discernment can lead to a new awareness of the Lord. Prayerful concentration on seeking his will may not bring a precise answer to a question determined by the community but it may give it the experience of a redeeming presence; a far greater gift than a particular answer could be.

When we consider that the future of a religious community may well depend on its contemplative depths, a newly found, collective awareness of the Lord may be the beginning of a new lease on life.

THE GRACE OF HEALING

13. The dialectics of prayer and reflection may lead to the discovery of new graces, even unexpectedly; and, in any case, it has a healing effect on the community.

Indeed, when each in the community turns away from his own preoccupation and focuses on seeking and finding God's will, a convergence of intentions is created and a movement in a common direction is initiated. It is the beginning of a liberation from factions and selfish projects; it is a significant move toward creating a unity of minds and hearts.

When prayer and reflection come together the integrity of our nature is restored. Through prayer our being is rooted in God; through intelligent reflection our humanity develops. We become whole. We cannot have a better preparation toward a wise decision. Even the object of the inquiry becomes secondary when with joy we discover a new equilibrium in our being.

At times there may be unexpected results and the process may bring surprises. The community may find a new insight or a new strength that God had in store for it. Such an event, however, is exceptional. Our expectation should be more ordinary: the restoration of a broken community, or the strengthening of the same.

INCREASED PRUDENCE AND WISDOM IN A COMMUNITY

14. The sharing of information and insights benefits all toward a better judgment and wiser decision.

Intense development toward a common vision and unity of purpose can be expected from a well-managed communal discernment process provided each person partakes in it ready to give what he has, and ready to be enriched by others. Then each is raised toward a better judgment and decision; and with the help of all each undergoes a purification of his insights and motives.

Discernment in community becomes a process of

building and of liberation. It is a building process. The available information needs critical examination to become worthy evidence. Unsubstantiated facts must be discarded; incomplete data must be completed. Insights must come from many directions and must be adjusted to the facts with utmost precision; otherwise they lead to fantasies and not to the understanding of those facts. Some insights must be trimmed; they go beyond the evidence. Some must be extended; they do not take into account all the evidence. Eventually the community must come to grips with reality by making a firm judgment on the desirability of an option. Indeed, this is building a unity of minds and hearts. Each must make his own contribution; each must be restrained enough to let others contribute too. It is building with precision, progressing continually in finding the right measure between two extremes: achieving less than what is needed, and construing more than what is warranted.

To achieve less means to overlook present complications and to ignore future consequences. It is an escape from whole truth, therefore disastrous. To construe more than what is warranted is another way of being unfaithful to facts; it is being in the clouds without any support from the ground. Theories that go beyond the evidence lead the community into a world of fantasy. No one will be able to stay there for long; dream castles are doomed for destruction.

Prayerful deliberation is also a liberation process. Each is helped by the others to progress from blindness to the perception of facts, from prejudices to good judgments, from reluctance to make hard decisions to the acceptance of the right option. The ascent to wisdom is also the ascent to freedom.

Such building and liberating activity, even when

focused on one issue, ordinarily requires far more than the honest and prayerful consideration of the arguments in favor of or against a course of action. Dialectical consideration of the opposites can certainly be of help, especially of initial help, but more positive work is needed. As in building a house, ultimately the strength and beauty of the construction come from the precise contribution and complex cooperation of all concerned: the architects, engineers, decorators and others; so the building of a wise decision requires a great deal of careful pooling of all resources well beyond the scope of dialectics.

THE QUALITY OF THE FRUIT DEPENDS ON THE QUALITY OF THE TREE

15. Ordinarily, the outcome of the discernment process, the final judgments and decisions correspond to the potentials of the group.

There is an analogy between the potentials of a person and of a community.

The potentials of a person are limited. No one can reach beyond himself, beyond his gifts of grace and nature, as no tree can bear fruit beyond its capacity. The potentials of a group, too, remain limited, even though it is enhanced by the presence of the Risen Lord. The most one could hope for is that the members will be lifted up to the best judgment, to the wisest decision given to any of them. Such fruit requires the conversion of the whole community to the very best insight and desire found in the group— an unlikely event in ordinary circumstances. We even doubt that such conversion is desirable. Each member

[41]

must develop at his own pace; he must grow slowly toward deeper insights and more dedicated options. Dramatic group conversions happen rarely; and they should not be forced.

In truth, it is too much to expect that in the course of communal discernment, the best judgment will always prevail. Our salvation history shows abundantly that prophets who were given a message from God often remained a voice crying in the desert. The community was slow to grasp their message; or at times was even downright opposed to it. True prophets are often lonely persons, appreciated more by posterity than by contemporaries. It follows that the legitimate expectation as the fruit of a communal discernment is rarely the emergence of what is best in the group, but rather the standard that the majority of the members can reach and grasp. A modest accomplishment, maybe, but a real one. We should not be disappointed. If we watch a group of runners, it is not a legitimate expectation to hope that all will keep up with the fastest one and reach the goal at the same time; the group achievement will be much less than that. If they all want to keep together, the fastest runner must slow down. The achievement will not be in speed but in unity.

Admittedly, such material analogy does not do justice to a spiritual situation. Nonetheless, it helps us to understand one precise point: it is unreasonable to expect that the objectively right but complex judgment and objectively right but hard decision will always gather consensus. Quite simply, many in the community may not have the disposition to understand the complexity of the question or may not have the strength to face the necessary harsh option. Indeed God may not want them to do so here and now. He is the God of patience and forbearance. His pedagogy throughout the time of the Old and New Covenants has been to introduce his people step by step into the fullness of truth and love.

To sum it up, judgments and decisions at the end of communal discernment will display human limitations.

This is not to deny the value of Christ's presence. In spite of the inherent limitations, it is effective. It brings more light, more strength to the community, but in the Lord's own slow way. It helps the pilgrims to progress on the road, but it does not imply a promise that at no time will they make a false step.

We do not know with precision how the Lord's presence operates, but we do know by faith that it brings a mysterious and mighty help to those who are gathered in his name.

ONE STEP FORWARD IN THE SERVICE OF THE LORD

16. The best and most legitimate expectation is that through discernment the community takes a step forward in the service of the Lord.

The community is God's pilgrim people. He leads them step by step toward the Promised Land. Such a pilgrimage may include events that are analogous to those recounted in the Bible: the flight from Egypt, the hurried wading through the Sea of Reeds, the confused and seemingly aimless wandering in the desert, the perilous conquest of the Land against fierce resistance, and finally, the day by day work of sowing the seed, planting vineyards, threshing the wheat and treading the grapes. The modern pilgrimage no less than the old is a journey into the unknown among many uncertainties. It requires much patience! God has his own ways and his hand cannot be forced. Communal discernment is not meant to lay the future bare. Jesus gave no such power to his disciples.

Rather, Jesus stressed that the life of those he sends to announce the Good News will be full of uncertainties. They must be prepared to be as defenseless as sheep are among wolves. Even if some good people will open their house and offer them hospitality, others will not. Often the disciples will be insulted, attacked and expelled from the locality; their life will be in jeopardy. When this happens they flee to another place. Throughout their perilous journey they will not be able to see the future laid out for them. The assurance given to them promises no less and no more than God's tender care and protection.

Community discernment then is not a means to know the future. It has a different purpose: it helps the community to become aware of the next step and gives them the strength to take it, be it through the desert, be it in the battle, be it in carrying out the mandate of bringing the good news to all men. To find the next step, limited as it is, can be correctly described as finding the will of God.

"WILL OF GOD" – WHAT DOES IT MEAN?

17. The expression "will of God" carries many meanings, numerous enough to trap the unwary.

An attempt to analyze what "will of God" means,

immediately recalls subtle distinctions between God's positive will and his permissive will. It recalls also bitter disputes between Dominicans and Jesuits who locked themselves for so long into the wrong question about divine initiative and human freedom. Our purpose here cannot be to undertake a full analysis of past subtleties. But past animosities should caution us of the danger of falling into a similar trap. We should remember too, that many saints did not have or need a scientifically elaborate concept to seek and to find God's will. Their progress did not depend on sophisticated theology.

Nonetheless, some pitfalls should be known; after all we do not have the sure instinct of saints. Therefore, some clarification of the idea of "God's will" is necessary.

One mistake would be to assume that we have to discover a precise plan, a blueprint drawn up by God for every move in our life. No, his providence does not work in that way. The details of a plan somehow emerge out of our own resources of nature and grace. God seals them by making all events work to the good of those who love him. "We know that by turning everything to their good God cooperates with all those who love him, with all those he has called according to his purpose" (Rm 8:28).

Another mistake would be to assume that God has no plan for us at all. He would be like a father who, once the child reaches adulthood, tells him, "Go your own way; I have nothing to say. You will have to make your own life." Such analogy is mistaken. God is a good friend who throughout our life has a plan for us. He reveals it step by step, calls us to follow it through gentle inspirations, hard awakenings, through all that ever happens to us internally and externally.

Between those two extremes we must find our

way. At one time we must create a decision after grace-filled and intelligent deliberations. At another time we have to ask for light and strength that we cannot muster in ourselves. Granted, there is something new in all decisions, whether they are created from our ordinary resources or are the extraordinary gifts of God. But in one case the fruit is produced out of the ordinary potentials of the tree; in the other case God's intervention produced the fruit that the tree could not bear.

To conclude, it is legitimate to expect that through discernment the community finds God's will, provided it is understood that in the pragmatic order this means simply the next step by the pilgrim's group in the service of the Lord.

THIRD QUESTION: WHAT IS IT THAT THE COMMUNITY SHOULD NOT EXPECT?

RESPECT FOR GOD'S FREEDOM

18. No community has a right to put a question to God merely at its own good pleasure.

If the dynamics of the discernment are toward the discovery of a grace that God offers to the community, there must be some previous inspiration from God to put them on this search. The instruction we received from the Lord for prayer applies to discernment too: "Truly, truly, I say to you, if you ask anything of the Father, he will give it to you in my name. Hitherto you have asked nothing in my name; ask, and you will receive, that your joy may be full"

(Jn 16:23-24). Such prayer is powerful even beyond the one that can move a mountain, since it brings an infallible response from the Father of all in all cases. But the interpreters of the Scripture agree that such prayer of petition must be inspired in the first place by the Spirit of the Lord; otherwise the promise does not hold. It must be a prayer for the coming of God's eschatological Kingdom, his reign in the heart of man.

Discernment is, after all, a form of prayer; a question transfigured through grace into a petition. The response of the Father can be expected if the question comes from the Spirit. Then the inspiration of the Spirit and the response of the Father are two distinct moments of God's continuous revelation to his people.

It follows that the members of a community intent on discernment must be deeply united to Christ, not only to find an answer to their problem, but to ask the right question in the first place. This applies especially when the community is moved to discover a new gift that is virtually equivalent to an extraordinary revelation, as it was in the case of the first Jesuits who deliberated about founding a new religious order. God guided them toward the formulation of the right question from early times when they first experienced the call of the eternal King; later when they enjoyed the consolations of their fraternal union; and finally when he inspired them to offer themselves to the pope, so that he might send them wherever the need was the greatest.

Even when the process of discernment is not intended to lead up to a revelation that can come only from God, but rather to the creation of an intelligent decision out of ordinary Christian resources, the question must be formulated with as

[47]

much wisdom as is expected to be in the decision. The wrong question, especially when it is put in the clear-cut dialectics that allows only for an answer of yes or no, can lock the community into an endless and fruitless search. Worse still, ordinary consolations and desolations may be associated with the wrong question, then taken as signs from God to confirm the community actually moving in a wrong direction. It follows that every community discernment should begin by asking if the question is the right one.

Moreover it is not enough for a question to be the right one logically; it must be moved also on the right level. Let us explain by an example. Ever since the Council many religious communities have grown concerned about the meaning of poverty. They raised a good question but often they handled it on the wrong level. Workshop followed workshop and sincere persons were flying from one end of the country to the other to find an intellectually satisfying answer. Over so many years the progress in understanding was minimal if any. The reason for such frustration is that the question of poverty should be moved on the practical level and according to the circumstances of each community, since the response must reflect the right use of created things for the specific purposes of the community. The solution must be worked out in practice. And to work it out is a weighing and measuring job; the right result can be reached through trial and error only. No community is really deprived of those resources that are necessary to find a practical answer.

It is quite possible that by debating the question about the definition of poverty, a community is trying to avoid—unconsciously perhaps—the real issue. To try to understand is a fascinating enterprise;

it can go on for a long time; many things can be left undone in the meantime.

GOD COMES AT HIS OWN TIME

> **19.** To fix a date for God's extraordinary intervention is to tempt him; to set a day by which ordinary deliberations should be concluded can be wise planning.

Life processes do not tolerate a rigid framework. If they are strong and aggressive, they destroy artificial limits; if they are weak and tender, the limits destroy them. Whether we intend to discover the delicate movements of grace through the interplay of all the members of a community, or we want to come to a creative decision, it is no more realistic to set a precise date for results than to fix the day in advance for the perfect fruit of the tree. This is not to suggest that the process should be stretched out without limits; it is to say that due respect should be given to the slow work of nature and grace. A good gardener knows how to wait for the sun and the rain and how to determine the best time to pick the fruit.

A further qualification is necessary. When the community is moved by the Spirit toward asking God to reveal to its members what they cannot know ordinarily, they are not in a position to impose a limit or deadline on God's mysterious ways by setting a date by which he must speak. Indeed if the example of the first Jesuits is invoked, their patient waiting through so many months for light, their flexibility in the method of their search, should be pointed out as well.

[49]

But when it is clear that the answer to the question must arise from the ordinary resources of the community, it may be wise to set a tentative date by which the deliberation should be concluded— provided, however, that such a limit does not interfere with the life process. This is not an idle remark; we have seen many times how the temptation to reach a decision can interfere with the quiet play of living forces. The temptation is all the more alluring if the participants believe that with some effort a decision can be reached by a given date. All that is necessary is to put pressure on the group by telling them that they must produce proposals by a given time. To avoid embarrassment and ill-feeling they will do so. The resulting decision will attract praise for efficiency, but there will not be much internal goodness in it. The relief and euphoria after such a process will be followed duly by the bitter taste of the immature fruit. It may be wise to set a date tentatively; it may be even wiser to cancel it.

NO LASTING SUCCESS COMES FROM A FORCED CONVERSION

20. The conversion of an individual person, as well as that of a community, cannot be produced at pleasure.

Every community discernment is a conversion process as well, since it is a movement to the better understanding of the Good News and to a more radical following of Christ. Such change requires renewed vision and determination. But persons as well as a community need time to broaden their horizon and even more time to adjust themselves practically to the new landscape. After all, human development is subject to complex laws. It is fed by the free acceptance of new ideas and by free choices of new courses of action. Such newness cannot be forced on anyone; it must be assimilated inwardly. More often than not, we have to wait patiently while the process of conversion progresses.

Since in a discernment process each member of the community is helping the others, they should all be aware that to promote or to assist the conversion of another is a difficult art.

First, all who take part should become aware of their own need for conversion. A feeling of self-righteousness excludes all progress.

Then each and all should recall that strong differences of opinion on a given issue frequently are due to different points of departure. If this is the case, to discuss arguments for or against a solution is a waste of time, since the differences on that level are merely manifestations of differences in foundational principles, be they theological, philosophical or psychological. The community should rather reflect on the origins of various approaches and see if any mutual understanding and respect can be achieved at some deeper level. At times, persons or groups have to retrace their intellectual views and moral decisions to the original starting points. This may mean that each individual must dismantle a great deal before the community can build something together.

Finally, when a unity or mutual understanding about the foundations is achieved, the community should face the real issue to be discerned.

Many conflicts in the Church after Vatican Council II are due not so much to different opinions on a

[51]

given issue as to differences in theological, philosophical or psychological foundations. The conflicts, of course, arise around a topical issue, but they remain unresolved. A climate of bitterness and sharp argument easily appears. When this happens there is a need for convergence of views and purposes before any kind of agreement can be achieved.

At times the proper fruit of discernment in religious communities should be in simply discarding the issue under consideration, coupled with a decision to dig much deeper and to discover the different foundations on which the mental and moral outlook of each person is built. When the participants know each other's starting point better, they may be able to construe new questions in a spirit of mutual understanding.

INTELLIGENCE PLAYS A ROLE

21. Communal discernment is no substitute for critical intelligence.

In all cases, critically trained intelligence is a good instrument to buttress spiritual discernment. In some cases, it is indispensable.

Spiritual simplicity can lead far in the city of God. But when the issue concerns the city of man as well, ordinary human prudence must be brought to bear on the problem and must serve as an indispensable framework in which spiritual intuition operates. No less a contemplative than St. John of the Cross warns repeatedly that we should glorify God by the full use of natural faculties before we ask for his supernatural intervention. Indeed God gave us intelligence to be used, and to be used fully. He will not give spiritual enlightenment when the light of intelligence is enough.

Let us stress this point because there is an anti-intellectual trend in the Church, particularly in the field of spirituality.

Christian wholeness does not consist in by-passing the intelligence in pursuit of holiness, but rather in a healthy integration of our humanity with God's grace. Especially when the subject matter of discernment is partly sacred and partly secular, our intelligence has to play a role and work as far as it can go. So called "spirituals" can cause harm to the community by playing down the role of intelligent inquiries. God is pleased with the proper use of his creation.

The more highly trained the human intelligence is, the more it glorifies God, and serves the cause of spirituality. To train the mind means principally two things: first, to enlarge its horizons, that is, to broaden the field of its operation; second, to discipline it to the point that its understanding and judgment flow from the facts available but never go beyond them.

The broadening of the horizon is a movement from childhood into adulthood, from naive simplicity into wise sagacity. A child is not able to place an issue in a broader context, for the simple reason that as yet he does not have an ordered knowledge of himself, of others, of the world he lives in, and of his Creator. Since he does not have many points of reference in his memory, he focuses on only one or two aspects of a complex issue. Then he judges—lucidly, and one-sidedly. He is misled by apparent truth, and he chooses what has the semblance of right.

[53]

The expansion of horizon is of course not completed instantly on the threshold of adulthood; it must go on throughout our life. Our judgment should improve with age as good wine does. Often, the success of discernment depends on the vastness of the field on which the mind is able to operate. Only God knows how much harm has been done to the Church by persons who prayed deeply but thought narrowly and acted accordingly. God did not work miracles to correct their mistakes. Rather, he used their deeds to keep the mystery of the cross present in his Church. But only God may do that; we are not called to contribute to the cross of others by well-meant mistakes. To avoid them, spiritual intuition should go hand in hand with trained intelligence.

Discipline of mind means fidelity to facts and to the rules of sound logic on the way to judgments and decisions. Therefore the solid foundation for communal discernment is in knowing how to use the mind and how to examine an argument critically. Also, each participant must do his homework on the issue at hand. Each must assimilate the problem personally and struggle with it. No one must consent to a decision unless he knows the data and has a thorough grasp of the problem. The communal presupposes the personal in the process of reflection. Each must retain his integrity, his faithfulness to the vision he can achieve, his commitment to the decision that is warranted in the circumstances.

CRITERIA FOR TRUTH

22. Consolations and desolations are not necessarily criteria of truth.

Consolations or desolations are signs of the disposition of a person before God. Since they are signs, and not reality itself, it is never easy to interpret them. St. Ignatius in his *Rules for the Discernment of Spirits* (*Exercises,* [313-336]) gives elaborate norms to help us to construe the meaning of these dispositions, yet he himself cautions us many times that deception or mistake is possible in the course of interpretation.

The basic principle of these *Rules* of St. Ignatius is akin to the teaching of St. Thomas on the knowledge of God and of things divine by affinity. Aquinas remarks that someone may come to a good knowledge of some precepts of Christian morality through sensing with the help of the gifts of the Spirit what is right and what is wrong, without ever having studied the matter conceptually. Ignatius affirms that a person who has grown in grace and wisdom responds positively to a movement of the good Spirit through experiencing peace, joy, courage, and so forth, and that he responds negatively to a movement that comes from the evil spirit by feeling restless, sad, depressed, and so on (see the *Rules for the Second Week*, [328-336]). Quite logically if someone is given to evil, his reactions will be the opposite. He will respond to evil suggestions with elation and to the inspirations of grace with a flight from his conscience that troubles him (see the *Rules for the First Week*, [312-327]).

Such rules are no more than an application of the Lord's saying that the sheep follow the good shepherd, for they know his voice (Jn 10:4). There is a continuity from the doctrine of John on the voice of the shepherd to that of St. Thomas on affinity and finally to St. Ignatius' *Rules for the Discernment of Spirits.*

[55]

In this doctrine of discretion or discernment, there are usually two aspects. One is in recognizing the quality of an inspiration and following it; the other is in coming to the affirmation of some truth, or of some value, either by accepting a proposition or by opting for a course of action. Communal discernment, too, has these two aspects. But at this point complications enter.

Consolations or desolations may be of help in discovering the divine truth. Indeed, St. Paul affirms that the experience of the Spirit leads to the knowledge of truth: "Now we have received not the spirit of the world, but the Spirit which is from God, that we might understand the gifts bestowed on us by God. And we impart this in words not taught by human wisdom but taught by the Spirit, interpreting spiritual truths to those who possess the Spirit" (1 Co 2:12-13).

But the proper criterion of truth in human affairs is compelling evidence. We have it when we know that all steps have been taken to find the facts, and to make the answer fit the facts. We have it when the answer covers all possible queries arising from the problem.

If we lose sight of this human aspect, it becomes impossible to reexamine the outcome of a communal discernment that involves judgments about human affairs. The criterion of truth would be in various spiritual impressions and not in solid reasoning. Such spirituality disregards God's ordinary creation and the reality of the incarnation, hence it is suspect. It follows that for a happy outcome of discernment, at least when any human affair is touched on, it is important to examine both the human reasons and the movements of the Spirit.

[56]

Also, the discerners should be aware that the judgments of the participants are not of equal value. Each moves within the limits of his own horizon, one narrow, the other broad. One remains within a tangible and material universe, the other explores the depths of the human spirit. Yet, each may report joy, peace and courage, even if his judgment is incorrect.

A similar consideration applies to every practical decision and option. None of us is totally free from attachment and bias. The degree of our freedom enlarges or restricts our field of choice. There, too, every choice we make must be critically evaluated. Intellectual sanity is a good disposition for the Spirit!

Even if the whole community reports peace, joy and courage at the end of the discerning process, the common judgment or the decision reached may still be vitiated by the narrowness of the mind and the attachments of the heart. Uniform peace does not necessarily indicate the presence of truth or value.

If there is a conclusion, it is that the signs of consolation and desolation must be handled with care and interpreted with caution.

THE VALUE OF ENTHUSIASM

23. Enthusiasm can be a good driving force when it follows an idea well-grounded critically; enthusiasm can lead to disaster when it is not disciplined by rigorous examination of ideas.

This particular rule is no more than an application of an old saying among philosophers that has found its way into the *Exercises* of St. Ignatius as well.

The saying is "from an entirely good cause,

nothing but good follows, but the smallest defect is enough to produce an ill effect."

St. Ignatius writes "we must carefully watch the movement of our thought; if its beginning, continuation and conclusion is entirely good, intending nothing but good, a good angel must be the source of inspiration. . ." (Exercises [333]).

In spite of the different wording, we are dealing with the same fundamental principle. There will be nothing but goodness in the actions of a person if there is wholeness in him. Wholeness means a harmonious blend between his emotions from which enthusiasm springs and his mind which is capable of cool observation and evaluation of other movements. If there is no internal unity in the person and his warm enthusiasm runs independently from his cool mind, the result will be fragmentation. If there is only cold calculation in him but not the warmth of emotions, he will be as inhuman as a computer.

When a community meets to deliberate, it should watch this problem carefully. A group is not involved in the nitty-gritty or the harsh reality of the application of beautiful ideas. Therefore, a group can be easily swayed by enthusiasm and consider anything that looks good and beautiful as immediately suitable for our real and sinful world.

INFALLIBILITY AND FALLIBILITY

24. The discerners are not infallible. Hence the outcome of every discernment process is fallible.

After Vatican Council II, a curious shift has taken place in the Catholic Church, if not in theory, certainly in practice. The understanding of the infallibility of the Church, especially as it is manifested through the acts of the pope and of the bishops, underwent some purification; consequently it is interpreted in a more balanced way. But during the same years a new myth began to grow up that granted infallibility to persons and communities to a degree that was not given to the college of bishops or to the pope. This phenomenon is particularly noticeable in many American religious communities. But we cannot have it both ways. If we welcome a restraint on the part of the hierarchical Church in its reliance on the gift of infallibility, we should be even more restrained in presuming that we are infallible—singly or collectively.

The simple truth is that virtually any process of discernment by individual persons or by communities of Christians takes place in the context of fallibility, apart of course, from a solemn doctrinal declaration by an ecumenical council or by the pope; a rare event.

When God stirs a human being, the divine intervention takes place and it is experienced at a depth that is beyond our images and concepts. But it cannot stay there: the mysterious inspiration must be proclaimed. But proclaimed it can be in a human tongue only. At times the proclamation comes confused and not intelligible, as in the case of the "glossolalia" mentioned by St. Paul (1 Co 14:1-19). Ordinarily, however it should be articulate and intelligible through words and concepts that carry a meaning for the community; it should be in the form of "prophecy" as Paul called it. Through such "prophecy" a mysterious movement initiated by the Spirit enters our own limited world, our culture, and our history;

[59]

the ineffable takes on a human form. But this human form is given the inspiration by the person who receives it; he gives it out of his own mental resources. As he expresses the meaning of the movement of grace, he also interprets it. In the final result, side by side with divine wisdom, there will be a markedly human contribution. The ineffable at the depth of the person and its articulation in human words are welded into a unity. God's clarity and human fallibility are there together.

It follows that no person and no community can claim that they articulate the movement of the Spirit in its purity. The most they can do is to proclaim their conviction that they believe they have been prompted by the Spirit and that they reached the best interpretation they could give to what was ineffable. The biblical story of Jonah, who received a genuine mandate from God but interpreted it in his own way, should be a salutary warning to all discerners. Jonah obeyed the call and announced, as he was instructed, that in forty days Nineveh would be overthrown. But the horizons of his mind were too narrow to understand that God could repent of the evil which he had said he would do to the people of Nineveh. When God did not do that evil, it displeased Jonah exceedingly, and he was angry. The story ends beautifully by describing how through parables and signs God helped Jonah understand that the pity of God can extend even to the hundred and twenty thousand heathens of Nineveh.

The Spirit of God present in the Church guarantees that the message given to men through Jesus Christ will never be lost, and that God's people will find their way to the Kingdom. Surrounded and protected by this exceptional certainty, Christians must live with fallibility in all other cases.

To understand our true condition leads to liberation. No one needs to pretend that he brings God's own revelation. Rather, everyone must submit his insights to the good sense of the community, and ultimately to those who have the final authority to judge; namely, the college of the bishops and the pope, so that what is missing in one's vision could be completed by the ministry of the Church. Dialogue is possible in the Church precisely because we are fallible; we are not a community where each one is called to make final statements in the Spirit.

God never promised that each of us, or every religious group, would have the power to state the truth infallibly, but "we know that by turning everything to their good, God cooperates with all those who love him, with all those that he has called according to his purpose" (Ro 8:28). A surprisingly generous blank check: God takes care of our well-meant mistakes.

THE HABIT OF PRAYER IS NECESSARY

25. Prayerful reflection during communal discernment will not supplement for the lack of long years of devotion and purification.

A habitually prayerful person will discern better in a short time than a dissipated one praying at length over the issue. An analogy illuminates this principle rather well. A learned and experienced surgeon will operate better and faster on the patient than a medical student who is consulting the best authorities during the operation. Improvised acts cannot take the place of a skill built up over a long period. Discernment at its deepest level supposes the habit of contemplation that cannot be acquired over a few weekend workshops, intense as they may be. This principle applies as much to persons as to communities. It is of some importance that discernment should be made in a prayerful framework; it is of greater importance that those who discern should be prayerful persons. It follows that for some communities the right question is not how to discern an issue but how to create a habit of prayer, even if it takes years to do it.

CONSENSUS CAN BE A MIXED BLESSING

26. If consensus can be reached, praised be God; if not, let us recall that to disagree is Catholic.

Consensus is a fascinating idea. What is more beautiful than the whole community being of one mind and of one heart in the Spirit and agreeing to the same judgment that eventually leads to a common course of action? There are times when God gives such unity. The First Fathers of the Society of Jesus certainly reached it at the end of their deliberation about religious obedience. In a different field, the laws for papal election admit the possibility of choosing a new pope by common acclamation under the inspiration of the Spirit. Consensus is certainly possible in some cases. When it is there we have to acknowledge it, respect it, and rejoice in it.

But ordinarily consensus manifested in an identical judgment will not and should not arise. Although God created all men equal, he did not give equal gifts of nature and grace to each one; neither did he create them exactly at the same spot in time and space; nor did he impose on them a uniform pace in their progress toward human and Christian maturity. Hence in the practical order, rare will be the issue when, through internal conviction, all come to the same conclusion. The overriding rule is that no violence should be done to the intelligence and to the freedom of anyone. Rather, we should anticipate that the vision of each will be different, and so will be his chosen course of action.

It follows that at the end of a community discernment process it is reasonable to expect a diversity of opinions. Consensus of judgment can be a gift from God. But it can be a man-made fallacy, too. When it comes from above, it builds the community; when it is forced on each and all, it destroys the community.

There can be another type of convergence in the group. It is not in a common assent to the truth of the matter but a common experience of peace in relation to the proposed solution of a problem. Intellectually some may not approve of the answer; they may feel compelled to oppose it. They are ready, nonetheless, to accept it as the only possible one in their community, as the only one that can unify the community. A complex situation indeed! Some minds do not find rest in the truth because they did not find the truth. But all find peace in a solution because it appears as the next feasible step in the service of the Lord. Such convergence is legitimate but by its very nature is fragile. Truth is not negotiable. Therefore those who are convinced that a judgment is not true, a decision is not right, have the duty to prompt the community to search further.

[63]

Their peace should last only as long as they do not have a reasonably good opportunity to move the question again.

In general it is wiser not to extol the importance of consensus but rather to insist that those who live in a community must carry one another's burden. This burden includes less than perfect judgments, less than the best course of action. The bond of a community was never in identical judgments but in charity that covers a multitude of limitations and shortcomings. To find perfection in charity means to accept the wisdom of a legitimate majority, or at times to accept their lack of wisdom. We have to find peace not so much in perfection as in accepting an imperfect world. Some communities hurt themselves through an endless search for consensus. They never find peace because they are unable to consent to their own imperfections and limitations.

THE PARADOX OF PEACEFUL MISTAKES

27. To assess the value of the outcome of a community discernment process, we must keep in mind that the experience of peace and joy in the Lord is compatible with erroneous judgments and objectively wrong decisions.

This statement does not come as a surprise any more. It simply sums up much of what has been said before. It affirms again that the community is not infallible in any kind of process. Consequently sincere efforts of its members to reach the objective truth or to make the right option may fail. But such failure does not necessarily make them less acceptable to

God. He loves them and guides them through their failing humanity.

God never wants more from a human person than the step that he can take here and now. Once the person exerts himself and takes that step, God is pleased and the conscience of his servant is at peace.

The capacity of a person is limited. Intellectually he may not be able to think further than simple common sense judgments which are sufficient to settle daily issues but are sadly inadequate, even harmful in complex situations. Similarly, in his decisions and options he may be confined to what is right for his small world, but disastrously inadequate for the greater good of a large community or of the universal Church. How many such cases we have today!

There is an objective world outside of us with its own ruthless demands for truth and purposefulness. If our judgments and options fall short of it, a price will have to be paid sooner or later, in spite of the peace and joy we may experience.

The gist of this paradox is that God takes us as we are and, provided we honestly search for him, he is contented and shares his contentedness with our conscience. But the same God made this universe with its own laws, and for us to operate in it well, nothing less than truth and correctness will do; error and imprudence will have sad consequences—no matter how well meant they are.

Ideally, the discernment process should bring forth a fruit that is good under all aspects: it contains the objective truth, it prepares for prudent action, and it springs from subjective righteousness. In reality, it is not always so. An historical example will give more light on this point.

[65]

It would be difficult to find a more spiritual man in history than Saint Francis of Assisi. He left behind for his brethren a rule of life that was intended to keep their communities together. There is no doubt that the rule was the fruit of discernment in the fullest sense. Yet, soon after Francis died, dissensions arose, and the rule he left proved itself inadequate to keep the communities in good balance.

Saint Dominic was a spiritual man too, but he was blessed with a sharp sense for organization. Consequently, he initiated the composition of a rule of life that was both strong and flexible to guide his communities through the vicissitudes of centuries.

No one can doubt that both men discerned, both found peace in the result. But the fruit of one's discernment was less suitable for the purpose intended than the fruit of the other's. Hence the telling difference between the history of the two orders. The Franciscans went through many crises and were split into separate, autonomous branches because of the different interpretations of Francis' heritage. The Dominicans kept their unity throughout centuries, due to the organizational genius of their founder.

The application from personal discernment to communal discernment is obvious. The same general principles are valid and the same difficulties emerge.

Where do we go from here?

Keeping in mind the paradox, we can arrive at a better understanding of the meaning of such signs as peace, joy and the like in the discernment process. They are indicators of the relationship of a person or of a community to God. They are not proofs that a given judgment or decision conforms to the objective order of things or is the wisest one. No wonder; those signals are ultimately the signs of a good conscience and conscience concerns our relationship to God.

Once this paradoxical situation is understood it becomes clear that there are no short cuts through the laws of nature. The criterion for truth is in objective evidence, followed by the assent of the mind to a judgment. This process by the intelligence cannot be left out or watered down without penalty, not even in a discernment process. God made this objective world. We must conform to God's objective world if we want to give full glory to him. A similar consideration applies to options among many courses of action. They must be examined critically to find out whether or not they are leading to the goal intended, whether or not they are the right means to the end desired.

These reflections suggest caution in using discernment in those cases in which a critical judgment must be formed or the decision must be directed to a specific end.

Let us give an example again. A community can rightly use the discernment process to arrive at a decision about poverty in the life-style of its members. At the end, peace and joy could be good criteria of the right decision. But the community should be far more alert to the exigencies of critical intelligence and reasonable planning when they want to set up new structures. If they are not well versed in the history of religious orders, in the dynamics of human community, in the technique of planning, they will not even realize what is needed and will feel great spiritual satisfaction with bad structures. Morally they are unblemished; practically they are heading for disaster.

[67]

It follows also that the expression "finding the will of God" should be used with caution. As we indicated earlier, it would take volumes to explicate the complexities of the will of God as we can comprehend it. Yet for practical purposes a useful distinction can be drawn. At a given moment for us the will of God is that we should try to progress toward him, to take the next step in his service, even if that step is objectively mistaken. For God the interior disposition matters. But God also created the world outside us with its laws independent from us. If the action of a person does not conform to that objective pattern, no matter how well he means, disorder will ensue, human beings will suffer and institutions will collapse. Often enough such sincere and misguided actions were at the origin of crucifying situations within the Church.

It does not follow that discernment should not be used. It follows only that we should know that its greatest value is to reaffirm our relationship to God. It is not meant to give extraordinary revelations. Once the group is aware of this limitation, they have a precious instrument in hand.

It follows also that once the discernment process is concluded, its results should not be presented with the words of the Acts of the Apostles and Ecumenical Councils: placuit Spiritui Sancto et nobis: it seemed good to us and to the Spirit. Rather the community should praise God and trust that he will never let it be separated from his Son, Jesus Christ. Nothing else really matters.

[68]

FOURTH QUESTION: WHAT IS THE DIFFERENCE BETWEEN DISCERNMENT AND AUTHORITY; THAT IS, WHAT IS THE RELATIONSHIP BETWEEN COMMUNAL DISCERNMENT AND THE GOVERNMENT OF THE COMMUNITY?

Not unlike a human person who must live from internal resources and organize his life externally, a community must have internal inspiration and external structures. Community discernment by its very nature is concerned with internal inspiration. External actions are the proper field of government.

Moreover, even if ultimately all authority comes from God, the immediate source of inspiration and the origin of the mandate to govern are not the same. One is in consciences; the other one is in a legitimate commission given by the community or by its representatives.

It should be clear from the beginning that the two sources of authority, the spirit and the law, not only should not be opposed but should complete and balance each other for the good of the whole body. The question therefore is quite legitimate: What is the right relationship between discernment and authority?

THE MEANING OF AUTHORITY

28. Authority and community cannot be separated from each other no less than a central organ

> of the human body can be separated from the rest
> of it. As there is no body without a central organ,
> so there is no community without authority.

One purpose of this thesis is to discard forcefully a false approach to authority in community; another is to give a succinct but substantial explanation of how authority arises and operates in a community.

We want to discard a false approach, common in the past, not rare in the present. It opposes authority to community as if they were two distinct entities. In the past it manifested itself through an unduly sharp distinction between superiors and subjects; a terminology that Vatican Council II tried to avoid. In the present it betrays itself by stressing the difference between "the leaders" and "those who are led;" a language certainly not borrowed from the Bible. Yet verbal expressions, insignificant as they may look, shape the mind, and the mind creates practical attitudes. Indeed, in the practical world, authority and community are often opposed to each other.

In a healthy community the two are organically united; one cannot exist without the other. Authority is the central organ of the community; its task is to create and to maintain unity in the group. Authority is not added to a community from the outside; it is a necessary creation from the inside. Nor is it opposed to the community: it is an integral part of it. Let us explain further.

A multitude of persons, even if they are together at the same place and in the same time, do not necessarily form a community. There are thousands of persons at Grand Central Station in New York City around five o'clock in the afternoon; yet who would claim that they form a community? They do not, because no bond of unity holds them together. If anything, they are rushing away from each other trying to catch their trains. A multitude of persons becomes a community when each is caught by the same vision, when each begins to do something for the same purpose. Then a near miracle happens: those who were many become one. Those who were rushing away from each other become united by common inspiration and common action.

But such a miracle in the group does not fall from heaven. There must be an earthly center from where the evolution is directed. Indeed it is necessary that someone should present a vision that fascinates the others; someone should point to a goal that all want to pursue.

Such a center of inspiration, such a source of direction is precisely what is authority. Its capacity to pull and hold the whole body together comes from power. It may be power given by the Spirit of God; it may be power that comes from human intelligence and determination; it may be power that is given legally by a larger community of which a smaller is part. But authority is rooted in power.

We should not be afraid of the word power. True, in modern English it may imply naked and brutal force, but its ancient Christian meaning is quite different; power means the strength of the Spirit in a poor human being. Such power is the foundation of all authority in the Church. Nowhere is this better expressed than in *Lumen Gentium* where the Council tried to explicate the deeper meaning of the authority of the Pope and the bishops:

> The Roman Pontiff, as the successor of Peter, is the perpetual and visible source and foundation of the unity

[71]

of the bishops and of the multitude of the faithful. The individual bishop, however, is the visible principle and foundation of unity in his particular church, fashioned after the model of the universal Church (23).

Further, since authority is the bond of unity, it cannot exist unless it is freely accepted by all those who are under it, or around it. Permanent and free dedication to the community holds the body together.

The interplay between the central organ of the body and the rest of it; that is, between those members of the community who are vested with power and authority and those who are not, is an ongoing interaction of living forces. Those in authority cannot function well unless they have the capacity to receive and actually do receive a multitude of ideas, suggestions, from all they claim to serve. If there is no such receptivity, authority ceases to be a living organ in the body; and, after all, what is the head good for if it does not receive impulses from the other members of the body?

Once the suggestions are received, those in authority must play their specific and crucial role. They must create a common vision and a common goal out of the multiplicity of ideas and purposes. To listen to all is a necessary step; without it the process of governing cannot even begin. But the task of authority does not end there: it must help all to accept a new unity.

Therefore the new vision ought to be communicated to all the members. Not imposed on them, but communicated to them in such a way that they can accept it out of their internal freedom. Thus the community becomes of one mind and of one heart.

[72]

Our consideration to this point explains the birth and the life of a community through the creative action of a center, or the birth of authority through the creative action of the community. The community forms itself by accepting and upholding a center of unity.

To understand authority even more fully, we must add that in the Church there is also a transcendental source of unity: the Spirit of God. The members of Christian communities are drawn together by the internal inspiration of the Spirit alive in each, and by the word of God spoken to everyone. The Spirit and the Word are one source of life for all; they are the ultimate rule and measure of all actions of the head and of the members. Truly, we can speak about the authority of the Spirit and the authority of the Word.

This steady relationship to God's Spirit and his Word distinguishes the ecclesial community from a secular association. In a democratic system of civil government the will of the people, manifested through the usual procedures of voting and electing, can be, indeed, in ordinary circumstances it must be, the norm of action for the government. In the ecclesial community the will of the people, no less than the will of those in government, is subject to the exacting demands of the Spirit and of the Word. Hence, the ordinary play of authority in the Church is enriched by a transcendental dimension where forces operate that do not have a human origin.

THE RIGHT USE OF AUTHORITY

29. Authority vested in man is a sacred trust. Even when its legal limitations are few its use is

**subject to moral and religious norms. Authority in.
an ecclesial community must be used for the sake
of God's Kingdom only.**

The center of power exists for the sake of the
whole body; to exercise authority is one of the
ministries in the community. Not one ounce of power
and might is given for the exaltation of the center; it
is entirely ordered and destined for the building and
strengthening of the whole body.

To achieve their mandate, those in authority must
have an absolute respect for objective values. Therefore, if they discover a gift in the community, e.g., an
exceptional talent for music in one of the members,
the right question for them should be: "How can this
gift be inserted into the operation of the whole
group?" We do not mean that the whole should be
adjusted to this one talent. But we mean strongly that
an individual and his talent should not be lightly
sacrificed to an abstract common goal. Admittedly to
strike the right balance that respects both the good of
the individual and the common good is not easy.

But the attitude of those in authority will be very
different if they look at a gift in the community as if
it were their own property, therefore freely dispos-
able; or if they look at it as a sacred trust that brings
with it the burden of fair accounting.

MODELS OF AUTHORITY

**30. Our understanding of authority underwent
serious changes in recent decades. Such changes
did not destroy what was good in the old**

conception but they corrected it, and perfected it, in many ways.

The reasons for changes are manifold. The world has become much more sophisticated. The standards of education have been raised and many religious communities have become the association of highly trained and specialized persons. The model of father-son or mother-daughter relationship is simply inapplicable in communities of highly educated persons. They all may be children of God but among themselves they are all grown up persons.

While to be in authority remains a distinct ministry, an indispensable one at that, it is not possible any more to point to the superior as the best-informed and most intelligent person, as a parent is for a child. He is as limited as the others are. Yet even in present day communities a center of unity is needed. If we must build it on a model, that of a "trusted friend" endowed with power to serve his brethren is the most suitable one. Communities should not be looked at any more as groups of children directed by a father or a mother, but as groups of friends who want one of them endowed with power to hold them together in faith, hope and love, and make their work more effective. The operation of authority as we described it earlier, is not possible if the parent-child model is followed; after all there cannot be a steady and fair exchange of advice between parents and children. Besides, there is something wrong when mature adults pretend that some of them are children. They should be as they are: children in relationship to God, adults in relationship to each other.

[75]

CHAPTERS DECIDE

31. At times the exercise of authority can be closely linked with communal discernment.

There are times when authority is assumed by the whole community, mainly for legislative and policy-making purposes.

The obvious example in religious life is authority exercised by a chapter. It could be a monastic chapter, where a small number of brethren consider an issue in prayerful context and come to a decision; it could be a general chapter where a large number of delegates from all over the world do the same. In either case, the preliminary process of praying and deliberating leads up to fully authoritative acts. The head and the members of the chapter; that is, the abbot and the monks, or the general superior and the delegates, reflect and come to a decision as one body. Authority is not vested in any one person but in a corporate entity, or in a college.

In such cases discernment enters into the preparation of a collective action. A hopeless conflict between the head and the members is not likely to develop since the structure would not let either side go on its own: as the monks could not deliberate without the abbot presiding, so the abbot could not preside without the monks being around him. Even if there are disagreements, the structures work in favor of unity.

THE COMMUNITY OFFERS ADVICE

32. At times the community may use the discernment process to offer qualified advice to those in power and authority.

[76]

We are entering the field of delicate operation, since we speak of a situation where the head and the members are not together in the discernment process; the members' prayers and deliberations are ordered toward an advice that will be offered to those who have the right to make a decision. This is a field that requires wisdom and restraint on both sides. Sharp conflict could come all too easily if the overriding desire of all concerned is not that of preserving unity.

When describing the nature of authority, we stressed that the members should bring their insights and proposals to the head. Each could do it individually after he prayed and deliberated alone. Or, all could do it collectively after they prayed and deliberated together.

Such collective process of discernment is feasible and conceivable but it can be successful only if every one realizes in the beginning that the community moves toward giving advice and not toward deciding. As always, the center should listen carefully. More than at other times, the center should reflect on what was said. But in truth he, too, can have the Spirit. Paul reminded the Corinthians forcefully, "And I too have the Spirit of God" (1 Co 7:40). The final decision should arise out of a dialectic play between the vision of the members and the insight of the head.

The situation is delicate because members may regard their advice as the final decision and they may try to force the head to comply. Or, the head may regard his own insight as the only right one and pay scant attention to the wisdom of many. Add to such natural inclinations the fact that we all are born in original sin and it is easy to see how a delicate play can become a bitter fight. There is no other way of safeguarding unity than by giving priority in all things

[77]

to humility and charity. If those virtues are strong on both sides no harm will follow and great good may be achieved. If not, the saying of Jesus will be fulfilled, "Every kingdom divided against itself is laid waste, and no city or house divided against itself will stand" (Mt 12:25).

INTERNAL INSPIRATION— EXTERNAL GOVERNMENT

33. In ordinary government it is wise to keep a reasonable distinction between the internal forum and the external forum. Prophecy and power to govern are two distinct ministries; they should not be confused, they build the body together.

Internal forum means the domain of actions known to God and to a person alone. External forum means the field where the ordinary power to govern operates in a community.

The conscience of a person is ruled by his vision and inspirations. The external life of the community is organized and directed by intelligent norms and precepts. The two fields should not be considered as opposed; rather, they should complete each other and together they should bring peaceful and purposeful times to the community.

Discernment is concerned with the world of conscience. The inspiration of the Spirit is sought, recorded, articulated, and given a meaning in such a way that the community can act on it. Government is concerned with good structures, with the coordination of activities and with the formulation of norms that help to build the best attainable harmony between the welfare of individual persons and the common good of all. The strength of a conscientious

[78]

decision comes from the internal resources of a person; the power to govern comes from a mandate given by the community, either through elections or by appointment.

A community is prosperous when there is respect for both conscience and government; when each of the two functions according to its own purpose without canceling out the other or supplanting the other. Neither of the two should be weakened; they should grow strong together.

How does all this affect the use of community discernment?

We have seen two cases. In the first one the community assumes all power; a decision on the external forum is made collegially by the whole group. It is right and just for them to use communal discernment as a preparatory process for the decision. In the second one, the community offers advice out of the resources of conscience to the ones mandated to govern. And thus, there is a healthy play.

There is a third possibility that must be handled with the greatest of care. The whole community, head and members come together to deliberate over an issue. In the process they intend to use the resources of conscience through discernment; but they move also toward a decision of government without the group as such being invested with external authority. At times all may go well: a good decision is reached that springs from good inspiration and can be put into effect by those in authority. No problem with that! At times, however, conflicts may develop. What is claimed to come from conscience may go against what is the aim of government. Such conflict situations are difficult to handle and may lead to disintegration.

Of course, in *Utopia* such conflicts do not happen.

[79]

There a decision inspired by internal faith and love coincides with the avowed goals of the government; but in a sinful world, such as ours, (and we have no other) such perfection is hardly ever reached. If it is reached it cannot be sustained for long. Overall, the role of conscience and the role of government are best kept distinct—as two vital organs of the same body are distinct. When their functions are confused conscience cannot correct government and government cannot uphold conscience.

Granted at times a king can be a prophet; nonetheless, ordinarily the role of David, the king, should not be mistaken for the role of Nathan, the prophet. The all-too-human history of religious communities supports strongly the need for a distinction between internal inspiration and external government. Confusion in the beginning is usually followed by conflict. The conflict is often resolved by the power shifting too far in one direction. Either the community becomes so powerful that it destroys effective government, or those in authority, in order to resist pressure from others, increase their power to an excess that weakens the whole body.

We are really not advocating anything else than healthy unity in diversity—so much esteemed by Saint Paul:

> Now you are the body of Christ and individually members of it. And God has appointed in the church first apostles, second prophets, third teachers, then workers of miracles, then healers, helpers, administrators, speakers in various kinds of tongues. Are all apostles? Are all prophets? Are all teachers? Do all work miracles? Do all possess gifts of healing? Do all speak with tongues? Do all interpret? (1 Co 12:27-31).

[80]

DAY BY DAY GOVERNMENT

34. While community discernment can fulfill an important purpose when the community is on the crossroads, its value for ordinary government remains to be proved.

In the history of every community there are times when important decisions must be taken since the community has come to crossroads. Those are indeed times for prayerful deliberation. The Hebrews had to stop to reflect and to pray after they escaped from Egypt and before they began to turn toward the promised land. They had an ideal setting for discernment: the desert of Sinai with God's mountain in the background!

Yet, great and valuable spiritual instrument, as communal discernment is, it may not be suitable for deciding about everyday issues, trends or currents.

Indeed, historically an informal procedure of discernment never functioned for long, as far as we know, as an ordinary form of government. If it existed, after a short while it gave place to an orderly decision-making process through discussions, deliberations and counting the votes. The informal procedure of the Council of Jerusalem developed into formal structures in later Councils until at Vatical Council II computers were brought in to count the votes and thus to help to assess the movement of the Spirit with some speed and accuracy. Nothing wrong with giving a spiritual purpose to a machine built with human intelligence!

In religious communities too, a similar evolution has taken place. The early simplicity of the brethren, whether they were monks, mendicant friars, or regular priests, developed into a more structured type of government in the form of chapters, congresses or congregations that work according to well-defined rules. The law of evolution is that enthusiasm is followed by structures. Institutions give historical stability to a fragile inspiration but there is a price to pay: the loss of freshness and flexibility.

Each community should have the wisdom to know in what circumstances it should turn to discernment. A precious instrument can be destroyed when used at the wrong place in the wrong time; yet, precious values can be lost if a good instrument is not used at the right place in the right time.

DELEGATION AND SUBSIDIARITY

35. As a person in authority should not hesitate to delegate his authority to expedite business, so a community should not be reluctant to delegate the process of decision-making and discernment to a smaller group, precisely to expedite business and also to free the members for effective apostolic work.

Unwise persons in authority try to concentrate power in their own hands; since they do not let the members share in responsibility, they weaken the body. Wise persons know how to delegate their authority, and by doing it they strengthen the body. The same principle is valid when it comes to community deliberations and decisions. An unwise community tries to reserve all decisions to the whole body or to a large section of it; consequently they overburden everybody. They favor interminable discussions and dialogues that are not in proportion to the importance of the case. A wise community selects a few proven persons and let them study the issues, produce insights, suggest decisions and options. They put into practice the principle of subsidiarity: what can be done by a smaller group, should not be done by a larger one. A way of conserving the energies of the community for prayer and apostolic work.

FIFTH QUESTION:
WHAT PRACTICAL GUIDELINES FOLLOW
FROM OUR THEOLOGICAL REFLECTIONS?

The following practical guidelines do not contain new insights. They suggest practical attitudes and actions for communities intent on discernment.

1. A community intent on discernment should recall the words of the Lord: "For which of you desiring to build a tower, does not first sit down and count the cost, whether he has enough to complete it?" (Lk 14:28). Its first resolve should be to keep the height and width of the tower proportionate to its gifts of nature and grace.

2. A community should not imitate any historical model of discernment literally unless the members' own circumstances are identical or very similar to that model, and their own resources are as abundant as those whom they follow. Since the First Fathers of the Society of Jesus were a small and deeply contemplative community, formed and trained by Ignatius for many years, and since they deliberated over an exceptional religious issue to which God only could give a reliable answer, their method and resources were unique, at least in part. The model needs to be adjusted before other communities begin using it for different kinds of issues.

[83]

3. While an ordinary community concerned with lesser issues may not be able to operate with such deep insights and such firm design as the first Jesuits did, its members should be perfectly able to find the next step in the service of the Lord. Therefore community discernment should never be presented as being unsuitable for a group of wise men or women who know their own limitations.

4. Communities are blessed by the Lord in different ways. The issues they face are different too. Hence adjustments in the method of finding the next step in the service of the Lord are always necessary. No pattern is universal.

5. In all communities peace is a fundamental condition for successful discernment. If there is no peace, a sincere search for reconciliation is recommended. It should be the only object of discernment.

6. The more a community is susceptible to being carried away by emotions the less it is disposed for genuine discernment.

7. To expect an answer from the Father is right when the question is put in the name of the Lord Jesus and is inspired by his Spirit. But no one should tempt God by raising a question out of his own resources and then postulating an answer by a fixed date. Such presumption has been abundantly condemned in the Scriptures. The community should know how to wait patiently when he alone can give the answer. Remember that no human effort can hasten his coming and that our impatience can easily lock us into a false solution.

8. When the community has the capacity to resolve a problem by using its members' own resources of grace and nature, it should not expect a

revelation but it should go ahead to find the best solution it can. The fundamental rule for any method is that all the exchanges and deliberations should be soaked in prayer.

9. The community can make good progress by focusing in prayer and reflection on each side of an issue, especially when the answer to a question must be a *yes* or a *no*. This was the method of the first Jesuits; it suited their purpose perfectly. And it may suit the purpose of some latter-day communities as well. But the method is not exclusive of other procedures.

10. When the question does not allow a simple *yes* or *no* as answer, other methods must be worked out that allow for steady, ongoing contributions from many sources. You must use different working methods for deciding the questions, "Should we build a tower?" and "How should we build it?" This distinction is particularly relevant for communities who are intent on writing constitutional documents.

11. While all should make an effort to understand and judge every point of view, all should accept also the onesidedness of a prophet and the penetrating but circumscribed insights of a genius. Many times in history a unique inspiration from God or an unusual insight into nature made a prophet or a genius unreceptive to arguments which seem good to everybody else. The community should treasure such persons. They make up in depth what they lack in breadth.

12. Throughout the process of communal discernment each member should participate wholeheartedly, both in giving and in receiving. If someone fails in either way, the whole body suffers.

13. Peace, consolation, and encouragement are

signs of God's grace and of his presence. They confirm the conscience of the community that is intent on taking the next step in the Lord's service. The objective value of such a step can be considered in two ways. First, in relation to the community: It may be the best for them because it is the most they can do. Second, in relation to other communities, including the universal Church and our human society: It may be good or bad; it may bring progress or disaster. An incompetent child can do his very best in driving a train and still cause it to derail and involve many others in the disaster. A competent man drives it properly and assures peace for all. This rule remains valid and is compatible with the belief that the presence of the Risen Lord enhances the capacity of the community to serve him.

14. The community should be cautious and remain realistic in its aim. It should not try to create *Utopia* here and now. When someone holds no responsibility for the practical execution of the decision, it is easy to be fascinated and carried away by perfection. Yet, what is perfect in the abstract can become destructive in the concrete order. The best can be the enemy of the good.

15. Community discernment should be an ongoing process. The actual time of discernment is no more than an intense period in the continuously evolving life of the community. Discernment must blend into a broader movement of life.

16. Community discernment must be a self-correcting process. When the community articulates what the next step is, there is a fallible human element in its judgment. It is subject to correction. Since our sinful condition makes our vision blurred, our insights limited, our decisions less than the best,

we must continually examine and reexamine what we have been doing.

17. In community discernment there should be room for dissent. Indeed dissent should be welcome and manifest for all to see. The dissenting voices of today are often the beginning of a new dawn for tomorrow. No one should be pressured into a common opinion. God loves persons in a community.

18. After the process of community discernment is concluded, it is wise to evaluate it. As an individual should reflect on his own thoughts and actions, so should a community.

The evaluation should not be done by the whole community but by a small group of trusted and qualified persons who have taken part in the process, or were present throughout it. They should report to the community.

To avoid any prejudice or bias, they should ask a number of objective questions. Here are some examples:

* Was every member of the discerning community thoroughly acquainted with all the relevant facts?

* Were they sufficiently learned and versed in the subject matter of the discernment?

* Were they given ample time for reflection, and for developing original insights, or did they labor under pressure?

* Were the participants peaceful, quiet and receptive?

* Was the climate prayerful?

* What role did critical intelligence play?

True answers to questions such as these may reveal more of the value of discernment than a diffused feeling of peace and happiness. Also, a community may want to follow the rule that it will not enter a

[87]

new discernment process until the last one is objectively evaluated.

19. Community discernment can be a powerful instrument of progress in the life of a religious community provided we do not expect wonders and miracles from it. It can assure quiet growth in grace and wisdom.

IN PLACE OF CONCLUSION

The conclusion to any study can have two dimensions. One emerges from looking back on the field covered by the author: a summing up of the questions and of the answers that succeeded each other in the process of reflection. The other dimension springs from a look forward beyond the field just explored.

The practical guidelines that we gave in the last part of this essay sum up sufficiently the gist of our questions and answers; there is no need to recall them again. Yet, we believe, there is a need to point beyond the scope of this study, even beyond all the benefits and blessings that communal discernment can bring. In doing so we take our inspiration from St. Paul. He wrote in his first epistle to the Corinthians:

> Now there are varieties of gifts, but the same Spirit; and there are varieties of service, but the same Lord; and there are varieties of working, but it is the same God who inspires them all in every one. To each is given the manifestation of the Spirit for the common good (1 Co 12:4-7).

All the gifts must be used for the common good; that is, for the good of the whole body that is the Church. The gift of discernment, too, when granted to a community, is given for the sake of a larger and more universal body than the discerning community itself. Indeed, a religious group reflecting about the next step to be taken in the service of the Lord can do so validly only when they look beyond themselves and their main goal is to build and to strengthen the

[89]

whole body that is the Church. Love and compassion for the Church of Christ is always the sign of the presence of his Spirit; as the lack of those attitudes is a virtually infallible sign of the absence of the Spirit of Christ.

But the gift of discernment is not the highest gift:

> And I will show you a still more excellent way. If I speak in the tongues of men and of angels, but have not love, I am a noisy gong or a clanging cymbal. And if I have prophetic powers, and understand all mysteries and all knowledge, and if I have all faith, so as to remove mountains, but have not love, I am nothing (1 Co 12:31-13:2).

Would Paul write today: "If I have the capacity to discern in all matters of heaven and earth, but I have not love, I am nothing"?!

At any rate all discerners should aim for the more excellent way: "So faith, hope, love abide, these three; but the greatest of these is love" (1 Co 13:13).

SELECTED BIBLIOGRAPHY

The purpose of this bibliography is to give the reader an orientation for further study. The books indicated contain ample references to other works necessary or useful for further study of the question of discernment.

* * *

Ignacio de Loyola. *Obras Completas.* Edited by Ignacio Iparraguirre, S.J. and Candido de Dalmases, S.J. Second ed. rev. Biblioteca de Autores Christianos. Madrid: La Editorial Catolica, 1963.
  The original Ignatian sources in a one-volume edition with numerous concise notes and references.
Guillet, Jacques and others. "Discernement des esprits" *Dictionnaire de Spiritualité ascetique et mystique. Doctrine et histoire.* Paris: Beauchesne, 1957. Vol III, pp. 1222-1291.
  A full theological treatise on discernment covering every aspect: biblical, historical, and systematic.
Therrien, Gerard, C.SS.R. *Le discernement dans les écrits pauliniens.* Etudes Bibliques. Paris: Gabalda, 1973.
  A scholarly work with ample references to relevant books and articles in the field of biblical studies.
Vries, Piet Penning, de, S.J. *Discernment of Spirits.* Translated by W. Dudok van Heel. New York: Exposition Press, 1973.
  An introduction into the doctrine of St. Ignatius of Loyola on discernment, based on original Jesuit sources.
Futrell, John Carroll, S.J. "Ignatian Discernment." *Studies in the Spirituality of Jesuits,* Vol II, no 2 (April 1970). St. Louis: The American Assistancy Seminar of Jesuit Spirituality.
Toner, Jules J., S.J. "A Method for Communal Discernment of God's Will." Vol III, no 4 (Sept., 1971).
Futrell, John Carroll, S.J., "Communal Discernment: Reflections on Experience." Vol IV, no 5 (Nov., 1972).
Toner, Jules J., S.J., "The Deliberation That Started the Jesuits." Vol VI, no 4 (June, 1974).
  All of these essays have been published in St. Louis by the American Assistancy Seminar on Jesuit Spirituality. They mostly focus on the practical aspects of the discernment process but contain also historical material.

THE THIRTY-FIVE THESES

1. Communal discernment in its best and purest form is the articulation of a contemplative insight into the working of God's grace in a community.

2. Discernment in its fullest religious sense is about truly great spiritual issues, where neither the simplicity of the dove nor the cleverness of the serpent is enough.

3. Communal discernment itself (as distinguished from the terminology) is not new in the Church; a careful reading of the acts of the Apostolic Council of Jerusalem reveals all of its essential elements (Ac 15:1-35).

4. Throughout the long history of the Church, there were outstanding examples of community discernment; the most important ones occurred in ecumenical councils and in religious communities, especially at the time of their foundation.

5. The process through which Saint Ignatius and his first companions arrived at the decision to form a religious community is a good model of communal discernment.

6. The message for our time coming from the early historical records of the Society of Jesus on discernment cannot be grasped accurately until the usual hermeneutical process of interpretation is completed and the past events are understood within their historical context.

7. Communal discernment is a good instrument of progress for lesser giants than Ignatius and his companions, and for lesser issues than the founding of a new religious community, provided that from beginning to end the members of the discerning group are aware of their limitations.

8. Communal discernment should be a process through which the community attempts to appropriate the best insight existing somewhere in the members, and make it into the community's own judgment. This is a correct description of what ought to happen; although it may not happen many times!

9. Ordinarily (not in its perfect form), communal discernment is a dynamic process in which the light and strength of God and the blurred vision of man all play their role. In it, a sinful community forms a judgment or makes a decision in God's luminous presence. The final result usually manifests something of all these ingredients.

10. The correct theological meaning of discernment is in the perception or discovery of a movement of grace, although the term is often used to include the procedural technique that best disposes a person for such discovery.

11. In a more subtle way another distinction can be drawn between two possible objects of discernment. It is a troublesome distinction, deceptively clear in theory, but always difficult to apply in practice.

12. For a community intent on praying, the most legitimate expectation is the presence of the Risen Lord.

13. The dialectics of prayer and reflection may lead to the discovery of new graces, even unexpectedly; and in any case, it has a healing effect on the community.

14. The sharing of information and insights benefits all toward a better judgment and a wiser decision.

15. Ordinarily, the outcome of the discernment process, the final judgments and decisions correspond to the potentials of the group.

16. The best and most legitimate expectation is that through discernment the community takes a step forward in the service of the Lord.

17. The expression "will of God" carries many meanings, numerous enough to trap the unwary.

18. No community has a right to put a question to God merely at its own good pleasure.

19. To fix a date for God's extraordinary intervention is to tempt him; to set a day by which ordinary deliberations should be concluded can be wise planning.

20. The conversion of an individual person, as well as that of a community, cannot be produced at pleasure.

21. Communal discernment is no substitute for critical intelligence.

22. Consolations and desolations are not necessarily criteria of truth.

23. Enthusiasm can be a good driving force when it follows an idea well-grounded critically; enthusiasm can lead to disaster when it is not disciplined by rigorous examination of ideas.

24. The discerners are not infallible. Hence the outcome of every discernment process is fallible.

25. Prayerful reflection during communal discernment will not supplement for the lack of long years of devotion and purification.

26. If consensus can be reached, praised be God; if not, let us recall that to disagree is Catholic.

27. To assess the value of the outcome of a community discernment process, we must keep in mind that the experience of peace and joy in the Lord is compatible with erroneous judgments and objectively wrong decisions.

28. Authority and community cannot be sepa-

rated from each other no less than a central organ of the human body can be separated from the rest of it. As there is no body without a central organ, so there is no community without authority.

29. Authority vested in man is a sacred trust. Even when its legal limitations are few its use is subject to moral and religious norms. Authority in an ecclesial community must be used for the sake of God's Kingdom only.

30. Our understanding of authority underwent serious changes in recent decades. Such changes did not destroy what was good in the old conception but they corrected it, and perfected it, in many ways.

31. At times the exercise of authority can be closely linked with communal discernment.

32. At times the community may use the discernment process to offer qualified advice to those in power and authority.

33. In ordinary government it is wise to keep a reasonable distinction between the internal forum and the external forum. Prophecy and power to govern are two distinct ministries; they should not be confused, they build the body together.

34. While community discernment can fulfill an important purpose when the community is on the crossroads, its value for ordinary government remains to be proved.

35. As a person in authority should not hesitate to delegate his authority to expedite business, so a community should not be reluctant to delegate the process of decision-making and discernment to a smaller group, precisely to expedite business and also to free the members for effective apostolic work.